PAY UP!

This book is dedicated to everyone who has either won or lost in Business and in Life through getting paid or not getting paid

PAY UP!

THE ULTIMATE GUIDE FOR CREDITORS AND DEBTORS

PATRICK ELLIS

WHO DARES SELLS Publications

Other books by Patrick Ellis:
Who Dares Sells
Pitch & Get Rich

ISBN 0-9512074-3-1

Every reasonable attempt has been made to ensure a high degree of accuracy throughout the book. The author regrets he cannot be held responsible for any unforeseen errors.

Published by **Who Dares Sells Publications**
12 Alexandra Court, Lampton Road, Hounslow, Middlesex TW3 4DL
United Kingdom

Printed by **Downey & Co (Specialised Printing) Ltd**
24 The Conge, Great Yarmouth, Norfolk, NR30 1JN, United Kingdom

Contents

Introduction

All too often in this day and age when you sell a product, service or idea, you have to struggle to get paid. Having done a decent job it can be soul-destroying to run into problems of not getting paid for the work you provide. In this book I explore some of the difficulties encountered in payment collection. I look at some of the ways others have managed to get their money out of non-payers and I also offer some effective guidelines on how to go about collecting what is rightfully yours. Some of the examples sail close to the wind and verge on the illegal. They are not methods to be used as they can often cause more trouble and cost more money and personal hassle in the long run. However, they do show how bad debt can anger, infuriate and drive people to take action they would not normally consider. If you are confronted by bad payers, **be tough** but **be legal** and follow the steps I outline to make people **PAY UP!**

Patrick Ellis
London 1994

Feast or famine?

Being in business can be a case of **feast** or **famine**. When the going is good and sales are plentiful and profits are soaring, businesses enjoy a feast. But they can and do hit hard times when customers don't PAY UP! The reversal of the situation from adversity to prosperity happens only when customers either pay voluntarily for what they have bought, or are made to pay by other means. Therefore in business you have to be both sweet and sour at different times, to keep moving forwards.

In the language of business, debtors are very powerful people — they can either make or break their creditors. So let us explore more deeply how to get paid in order to keep your business pressing ahead.

Debtors use various tactics to avoid paying their creditors — some are genuine, others are not. A number of ploys could be based on lies — to buy time, to make money by investing what they owe, or to deliberately avoid paying out — in other words, **fraud**.

Some of the classic answers debtors give their creditors are:

- The cheque is in the post.
- The product/service we bought is lousy.
- We've run out of cheques.
- The person who signs the cheques is off work.
- We didn't receive the invoice.
- I am too busy at the moment — I'll look into it and call you later.

- I am going on holiday.
- We only pay every 90 days.
- There is a management change.
- We haven't received the goods yet.
- Give me your telephone number, I'll call you back.
- We don't want the product or service (after making use of it).

There could be a host of similar stories either to put the issue of paying to one side or as a concentrated effort to deliberately not pay.

If creditors analyse some of the stock replies debtors give them, they will discover that they have:

- been too trusting by assuming the debtor would pay when required,
- been too lenient and unbusiness-like in their dealings,
- not made the payment terms clear to the debtor,
- believed the debtor could afford it, through the false impression given without double-checking,
- not taken out credit references,
- been naïve and assumed that all people are honest.

Therefore, before giving credit or extended credit to anyone, careful attention must be paid to the circumstances of each case individually.

The criteria that must be applied by any astute businessman before giving credit or extended credit to anyone should be based on the following factors:

- Do they have a good track record or payment history?
- Are they honest and trustworthy?
- Are they credit-worthy?
- Can I afford to give them credit or extended credit?
- Will it affect my business relationship if I am too hard and do not show any flexibility in this situation?
- Could I lose them to a competitor if I tighten-up and demand payments on time, every time?
- Why is their bank not helping them out?

- Are they going through financial difficulties? How long could it last?
- What sort of interest rate should be charged for any credit or extended credit given?
- What do I stand to lose if they default?
- What are my feelings towards taking court proceedings to recover the debt if all else fails?
- Should I use a debt collection agency?
- What do I stand to gain by being lenient to the debtor in the circumstances? i.e., What increased benefit is there for me in this in the future by treating them lightly now?
- What is their situation like with other creditors?
- Is the debtor's kind of business, generally speaking, in trouble?
- Would I be responsible for the debtor's downfall (possibly even suicide) by destroying their business and private life by making life hell for them?

Guidelines to safeguarding your payments

The following list suggests effective measures you can take to ensure you get paid. In a later section I discuss with a solicitor, specialising in debt recovery, some of these and other methods of protecting your payments.

1. Get a minimum part-payment before doing any work.
2. Work on a *pro-forma* basis with Cash On Delivery (C.O.D).
3. Get bank references plus two trade references (two of the suppliers).
4. If it is a large amount of credit, then get a credit reference (from an agency), i.e. a status report.
5. Your invoice must include the terms of payment. It must also specify the number of days in which the payment has to be made and state that the debtor is liable for costs incurred through payment collection procedures, if he/she defaults.
6. The "Retention Of Title" clause which also should be included means that the goods are the property of the supplier, until they are paid for in full or part.
7. Use a three-stage letter cycle to collect your money. The first would be a polite request for payment of the invoice (with a copy of it attached). The second letter

would be a demanding one, followed by a very business-like phone call. If payment is still not received, the third letter should be the "Final Notice" giving seven days to pay, with the alternative of facing legal action.

8. Take out credit insurance for peace of mind — it is better to have insurance and not need it, than to need it and not have it!

   Credit insurance protects a creditor's payments if the debtor does not pay because of insolvency or protracted default. It can be used when trading at home or abroad. Taking out credit insurance eliminates the risk of trading on credit with your customer.

   Whether you are dealing with a blue-chip company, or one that you know well and can trust, it is still a good idea to have credit insurance because the fact-of-the-matter is that no one is immune from bad debts or insolvency, which can be caused by a combination of adverse factors.

9. Try using factoring. Here is an explanation of what it is:

   Factoring is a £16,000 million-a-year industry. It is an effective method of ensuring your working capital reserves are kept topped-up when sales grow, and of meeting the demands this growth imposes for more funding for your business's needs, and also to safeguard against the likelihood of more debtors that could crop up with your increased trade.

   Due to difficult trading conditions, particularly in times like these, the banks have tended to tighten-up their lending criteria and have not increased overdraft limits or given business expansion loans easily.

   If a business does not get paid on time for the products, services or ideas it sells, this can cause a big problem for it. The answer to such a problem could be factoring and invoice discounting (a confidential method of factoring where the the client's customer is unaware of the factor's involvement) that the banks themselves provide through their factoring subsidiary: they provide immediate payment against any outstanding debt owed to their client if they consider the debtor to be a good business account. The cost of using the factoring system is charged around the overdraft facility mark. And factoring has its distinct advantages:

a. It increases proportionately with increase in sales.
b. You do not need a debenture to obtain it, i.e. you do not need a certificate from the bank saying you have a loan on which interest is payable.

The onus lies on the factor to collect the money from their client's customers in accordance with the client's trading terms and conditions and to maintain goodwill. To run the factoring business effectively, the factor has the required technology, systems and human resources and can therefore collect the debt in about 60 days — usually three weeks faster on average than the business on its own can manage without such facilities, thereby resulting in better cash flow and lower interest charges.
The threat of bad debt is always there. By using a full service factoring agreement, 100 per cent protection can be given by the factor to their client against bad debt on all approved business. However, a recourse factoring agreement does not offer this facility — if the debt is not paid by the customer, it is passed back to the factor's client.
All the big factors have access to libraries of credit information and therefore can give their clients quick and realistic approval on potential customers.
Factors pay their clients automatically after an agreed period of default. This is different from a credit insurance policy, where a formal claims procedure has to be followed. (*Source: International Factors*)

Even if you use all these safeguards and effective ways of dealing with the situation of getting paid, debtors can turn out to be very troublesome to handle, unless you also take a view from a different angle and have learnt how others have got paid when they were faced with the unpleasant task of collecting the money that was rightfully theirs. Some unsavoury methods used by desperate people to collect money owed to them might be seen in another light to be humorous, unconventional, risky and daring. Often they do produce the desired result, but they are not recommended — for good reasons.

The dilemma of getting paid

Get paid and survive, or go bust. That is a choice we are faced with. It is a trap we could get caught in. After you give your time, effort and money to a job of work, getting paid for it in return is what really counts.

All over the world, many well-meaning givers (sellers) get stitched-up by their takers (buyers) who receive the work and then will not pay for it. Alternatively they will find 101 ways by playing dirty to beat the seller down to a ridiculous figure, far lower than what was initially agreed.

The result is frustration, anger, ridicule and — more importantly — loss of income or revenue. This inevitably produces further anguish because it affects the giver's business, private life and future wellbeing. However, it leaves the taker gloating over the fact that he has taken yet another do-gooder for a ride. Unless the wrong done is confronted and dealt with, the taker will be allowed the false sense of "getting away with it"!

To put the matter right the giver could be involved in a costly court battle with further loss of time, money and effort and the possibility of the plaintiff getting judgement over the defendant, but in the final event the giver not getting paid his dues. The object of using the legal process is to recover the money, but a travesty of justice happens all too often. The law is truly an ass on some occasions. I speak from first-hand experience.

People who do not pay or try to wriggle out of paying are not necessarily crooks. They are more likely to be misguided opportunists, who need to be handled in a special way to get what you want out of them after they have got what they wanted out of you.

There is one remedy for getting paid without using the legal process, which is only recommended as a final resort. If you do have to use the legal process to get your money, do not put too much faith in it. I have interviewed many potential victims of debtors who managed to maintain their dignity and get the payments due to them without having to go to the courts, by using some commonsense, tough measures.

The remedy is this: I strongly recommend that, as well as this book, you read my other two publications, **WHO DARES SELLS** and **PITCH & GET RICH**, to acquire the knowledge of psychology and communication skills required to make you a champion at getting paid.

After you have read my three books you will end up with a master qualification on how to get paid — not a B.Sc. or a Ph.D., but you can call yourself Dr Pay Master M.O.N.E.Y., a "graduate" of the University of Real Life.

The restaurateur's story

In my research on the complexities of getting paid for the work I do, my first discovery about how someone, other than myself, got paid in his day-to-day business activities was when I was talking to a restaurateur. He told me how on the odd occasion he came across a smart cookie who ate and drank until his belly was full and then tried to get out of paying by complaining that the food was poor quality or the service was bad.

He then told me that on one particular afternoon that very thing happened. A smartly dressed drunk and his inebriated lady friend came in and ordered a feast, which was laid out before them with more drink — champagne!

After scoffing and burping away, the diners, when confronted with a bill for £135.00, started muttering under their breath, complaining bitterly that the food and service left much to be desired and they were not going to pay. The restaurant in question was a high-class establishment and the diners' objections were untrue.

The waiter immediately notified the restaurateur (who was the owner). His first reaction was to tell another waiter to shut the front door. He then instructed the

first waiter to go straight into the kitchen and bring a meat cleaver while he dealt with the troublesome pair, who were now getting abusive and noisy.

He walked straight to their table and said: "Did you enjoy our food, sir?"

The drunk replied: "No, the food and service were a f...... disgrace, and we are not going to pay."

The owner then said: "I am sorry to hear you say that, sir; would you prefer to try some hospital food instead?"

"What do you mean, you son of a bitch?" said the drunk.

By now the meat cleaver was in the owner's hand and displayed (only as a warning, of course!) to the troublemakers. The restaurateur was a karate black belt and could well take care of himself.

He then turned around to the drunk and said: "We have a good recipe for those who do not pay. We never call the police. We first call the ambulance service and then let them call the police . . . Now you either pay up, or else . . . You entered our restaurant smartly dressed, walking upright and talking big, but you will leave with our compliments quietly, flat on your back on a stretcher — not as a British dummy, but more like an Egyptian mummy, all bandaged up from top to toe. Get your money out now, you stupid man."

The drunk replied quickly: "Sorry, sorry, I didn't mean to upset you. Here's the money."

The restaurateur took the money, but in his infuriated state he lost control of himself, grabbed the drunk by the scruff of the neck and hurled him out of the restaurant, with his lady-friend following soon after. They both ended up on the pavement.

On the following day, when the drunk and his lady-friend regained their senses, they went back to the restaurant and apologised profusely to the owner for their bad behaviour, which he forgave and forgot. Those "drunks" eventually became two of the restaurateur's best customers and friends.

This was an extreme method which worked in that instance, but I would not recommend it.

A strategy for coping with non-payment

Here is a strategy you can use when someone refuses to pay.

1. Try to establish the cause. Is it genuine, a smoke-screen, or a deliberately crooked act?
2. If it is a genuine case, no matter how urgent your needs are, this is where wisdom comes in: show understanding. Getting cross with your debtor and threatening him with violence, legal action, etc., will not help. A person must have the money to pay you back in the first place. If he does not have it, no matter how hard you try or what method you employ, it will serve no purpose. You can't get water, if the reservoir has run dry!

   Instead, go one step further. Try to help your debtor to repay you, by recommending ways to solve the dilemma. In doing so, you will remove two problems in one stroke, both yours and his. You may possibly make a solid friend in the process.
3. If it is a smokescreen, you have to penetrate it to get to the root of the problem. The person has the money, but does not want to pay. You are advised to be a little brutish in your approach here. Ask awkward questions, humiliate, subtly threaten if necessary,

until the debtor admits the hoax and coughs up. When he/she pays up, praise him/her. Until then, play the adversary.

4. If it is outright crookedness, you have to show your debtor that you appreciate their skill in trying to put one over, but it is bad manners to try it on you. Tell them that had you not tumbled their game (i.e. what they were after) you would have gone to the police or fraud squad like a novice. That would have complicated matters. You should say that you are not that sort of person and that all you want is payment, and not to complain — so **Pay Up!**
5. If that has not made them respond, after you have given them a chance to be fair to you, tell them you are going to see your solicitor about it, and that your next meeting will be in court. This may very well scare them into paying up.

   Only if the amount you are owed is sizeable is it worth pursuing through the courts. That line of action is recommended only after you have exploited all other avenues and thought about it very carefully. Remember, to recover your loss through the courts could cost you even more and there is always a risk that you may not get your money in the end.

A sign in an undertaker's office read:

Face the inevitable. Pay now, beat inflation and have a trouble-free departure.

The builder's account: The struggle to obtain payment

My interview with self-employed builder Dave will shock you and also rock you with laughter because of the hassle he went through to get his money for work he did.

Patrick: Hello Dave, I was both troubled and amused to hear some of those experiences you had to encounter to get paid. It's something a lot of people like yourself also face. Can you relate a few incidents that you have been through in your business life and how you eventually got paid?

The Battle Of Britain

Dave: Sure. Well, one job I did was in Buckinghamshire. We did a fine job. Everyone was pleased, until it came to the point of asking for the money, when the customer said no, he wasn't going to pay.

I asked him why.

He said he was very pleased with my job as a bricklayer and plasterer, but he wasn't pleased with one of the carpenters.

I asked him what that had to do with me, and why he was penalising me?

He said that it had nothing to do with *my* work, but the carpenter's workmanship spoilt the job, and therefore he reckoned he wasn't going to pay anybody. I went home and thought about it. I was so upset that when my Missus put my supper on the table, I couldn't eat.

Patrick: You must have been terribly upset.

Dave: That's right. So I went around to his house that evening. I knocked on the door but he wouldn't let me in. He used to leave a window at the side open for us, where we could get into the house when he was at work. So I opened the window and in I went.

He started shouting at me, calling me all sorts of unpleasant names, but I told him when I had finished what I was going to do, I was going to cripple him for life; so he ran into another room.

He had just had his heating and skirting board done all around the house; so I destroyed that. He was a connoisseur of wine. He used to make a lot of wine, which he did in the back, and there were four vats fermenting, ready for bottling, so I pulled the covers off and urinated in every one of them. He wasn't very pleased. He then came at me again hurling abuse and I said, "If you don't come up with the money, the next thing will be your new Rover car."

Patrick: Was the man a crook?

Dave: No, funnily enough, it appeared he was just an ordinary, decent working man. He worked as a construction engineer for the Government.

Anyway, when he saw I was going for his car he called me into his room and offered to pay me. When I saw on his desk that he had the money there all the time, I just couldn't understand why he had to cause all this hassle. So he paid me my money, but the bad thing about it all was that he didn't pay anyone else.

Patrick: He had a track record of "doing" people?

Dave: Oh yes. Afterwards we found out that he got work done and didn't like to part with his money. He tried to live on your money. He used other people's money to supplement his income. He was clever, but not clever enough.

Patrick: Did you take any other action with this man before he paid you?

Dave: Yes. I poked a screwdriver in a pipe which was behind the ceiling, so that when the water was turned on, it would bring the ceiling down. I can't say if it did or not, because I never went back again. Once I got my money I was gone. But there are some terrible people about.

Then we had another instance where we tiled a roof for a colonel. He was a well-to-do man. He had plenty of money, but when we finished the job it was the same old thing again. He said he wasn't going to pay.

Patrick: Just like that?

Dave: Just like that!

Patrick: You mean he came out straight and said: "I am not going to pay you"?

Dave: That is right.

Patrick: You mean he came out straight and said: "I am not going to pay you"!

Dave: Yes. I am self-employed, and I've got a mort-

gage, the same as everyone else. I went back on a Sunday morning with a ladder. I put the ladder up at the house and started taking the tiles off. He came out screaming. He said he was going to get the police.
I said: "Well, you're not paying for these tiles. I've paid for them. The tiles belong to me, so I'm having them back."
He called the police. The police asked me what I was doing. I explained to them that I had tiled his roof, and paid for it out of my own money. I showed them the receipts. The man wouldn't pay for some reason, so I was taking

my tiles back. The police just left me to get on with it.

Patrick: Is that so?

Dave: Yes, it was a fight between me and him. After I took a few more off, he said that if I came back later he would pay me there and then, which he did.

Patrick: In other words, what you are saying is that if somebody plays dirty, you have to take some sort of direct action to recover your payment?

Dave: Yes, because you will find that a lot of people will have a job done and then they say they are not paying, or they haven't got the money, just to see what you're like. I mean, if you're silly enough to walk away, then they're laughing all the way to the bank.

Patrick: Correct. But don't you have a written contract for the jobs you undertake?

Dave: Well, sometimes I do, but most times I take their word for it and trust them. They trust me to do the job, and I trust them that they are going to pay me on completion. Understandably, if it is a bad job — yes, they've got the right to say they are not going to pay. But if everything is all right and they are pleased with the job, then I want my money. Otherwise I take action.

Patrick: **Who Dares Sells,** or **Who Dares Gets Paid!** Are there any other incidents you can recall?

A sledge hammer to crack a hard nut

Dave: Yes. There was a building contractor — I sometimes take work from a contractor with other builders — and I finished my job a little earlier than the others. This man was about 18 stone, and seven feet tall. He looked like a gorilla.
As he passed me he said: "I suppose you want

your money." I said: "Yes. I've done my job." And he said: "Well, you're not going to get it."

Patrick: Just like that?

Dave: Exactly. So I said: "Why?"
And he said: "Well, it's just one of those things. I'm not paying you and that's it." And he just laughed about it.
I thought to myself, well, he's a very big man. What can I do? He's bigger than me so I must get a weapon to make it fair, just in case he became heavy with me. So I picked up a sledge hammer. But, he happened to pass me as I was lifting the sledge hammer up, not to actually strike him, and it accidently hit his knee.

Patrick: You mean it was an accident?

Dave: Definitely. But he went down on the ground and swore blind that I went for him with the sledge hammer. I said I didn't, but he kept swearing that I did. He told me to leave and asked me to come round to his house at seven o'clock in the evening to collect my money.
Well, I was worried that he was going to have me when I went round, but luck had it that when I pulled up there I saw the curtains twitch, and as I walked down the pathway his wife opened the front door, threw the money at me, called me an animal, said I'd tried to kill her husband, and told me never to come back again. I picked up my money and off I went. Funnily enough, I met the same contractor about a fortnight later and he asked me to do more work for him. You just can't win after all.

Slippery customers

Patrick: Right. It appears from what you tell me that when you encounter the problem of people not wanting to pay, rather than trying to think it out and resolve it by talking, you have had to take physical action.

Dave: Yes.

Patrick: Why didn't you try to talk to them to resolve the problem rather than resorting to physical action?

Dave: In the past I have tried it, and all they say is, "Come back in the evening." You go back in the evening and they say they haven't got cash or they haven't got their cheque book, and you should come back another evening. And you spend a week going backwards and forwards.

By the time you finish you've spent more money than what you are owed, trying to get it back. It just doesn't make sense doing it that way. You know that they've got no intention of paying you when you carry on like that, so I take tough action and they pay up.

I once did a job for a director of a firm. Now, all it involved was two glazed tiles in his kitchen. I cut them out and re-did it for him. All I charged him was £5. The material nearly came to £5.

When I went back to his office and asked him for the money, he said: "I'll give you a cheque."

I said: "Surely you haven't got to give me a cheque for £5."

And he said: "Well, I don't carry cash."

Then he told me he didn't have his cheque book, and asked me to come to his home in the evening to collect the money. I went in the evening, but he still didn't have his cheque book. I went to his house four nights running to try to get £5. I lost all that in petrol and messing about.

In the end, I had to say to him that if he didn't

pay me the £5 I would tell everybody in the factory he didn't pay his bills. And then he paid the £5. And he paid it in cash. Why should you have to put up with them trying to make you look a fool, taking your money by not paying you?

Patrick: What you are saying to me is there is a devious streak in a lot of people, and no matter how sincere you are, and how well you do a job, you find people who will try to do you.

Dave: Definitely. But there are also plenty of nice people too, who want to pay you even before you start.

I have done many people's houses where they say: "How much do you want, Dave?" straight away.

And I say: "Well, let me do some work first."

I mean, you do find genuinely nice people. I find the working class people are good people at paying. It seems to be the ones who have got position and are living on a monthly salary, who just can't work it out.

Then you get the very rich, who are very nice too. You do the job, they're pleased, and they pay you the money. It just doesn't make sense.

Patrick: Are there any other useful experiences that you have had apart from these?

Dave: Certainly. It's just silly things. For instance you work for people and they say they're not going to pay you. You try to be nice about it, but in the end you can't be. You've got to be aggressive with them or you just don't get anywhere. What you're doing is going to people's houses, paying for materials, doing a job for them, and then they don't want to give you the money. How can you survive?

Patrick: On a larger scale, now that you are working for an employer, have they had any major problems recovering money?

Dave: Oh, yes. They have had quite a few. One debt was for £30,000 for work they did. The man who owed it bought a place in Spain and moved there. One of my bosses went over there to see him about the £30,000. He gave the boss dinner, and while he was having it he said: "When you've finished your dinner, get on the next plane and get out of here because you're getting no money." And they never did pay.

Patrick: Just like that?

Dave: Just like that. Another man took them for £25,000.

Patrick: But what do you think the law could do?

Dave: Well, I'll give you an interesting case. I now work for a main building contractor. The same colonel I was talking about earlier, who wouldn't pay me, had about £50,000-worth of work done through them. When they went in for their final cheque of about £30,000 or £35,000 he wouldn't pay it, so they took him to court. It took seven years to go through the court and they got nothing in the end. It cost them more, in the long run.

Patrick: I was done by a guy for £2,600 (which certainly is a rare occurrence for me). He was a restaurant owner — a charming man. Believe you me, the man lives in a very posh part of Middlesex. He drives a nice car and always dresses smartly in a three-piece suit. I took him to court as a last resort because he did not pay me my money after promising me faithfully to do so and then breaking his promise many times.

I had to get legal advice which cost me about £350. I got judgement against him. I sent the bailiffs in — and that cost me £40 each time to issue the warrant. The bailiffs went in there twice and I didn't get a single penny in the end. I subsequently got to know through the grapevine that the guy was flat broke and became an artist for the British Government — he was drawing the dole!

I lost £2,600 plus £350 on top of that making it £2,950, plus another £80 for issuing the warrants, which amounted to £3,030, and I see the same guy every now and then and he has the cheek to meet me and say, "Hello, Mr Ellis. How are you? How's business?" And I just grin and bear it.

It is diabolical, Dave, and I think I could very well have turned to the dirty tricks department and done similar sorts of things to what you did, or sent in the heavy mob to demand payment, as many have advised me to do. But I find it difficult to do that sort of thing, for the simple reason that I value human life and I am philosophical about both business and life . . . You win some and you lose some, and you can't win every time.

But I understand from people like yourself, who have been faced with similar problems and have dealt with them in the way you have described, that strong-arm tactics do work. What do you have to say on it?

Dave: I look at it this way. That man who owes you money, what if it was the other way round? What would he do? Wouldn't he use dirty tactics on you?

Patrick: Quite possibly.

Dave: Well, there you are. I mean, you can't just sit through life, and get stitched up like a kipper. I'm not a violent man. I don't want to be a violent man. I just want to go through life being happy. But when I go out to work my philosophy of life sometimes gets badly shaken.

Patrick: You go to work to get paid. You've heard

the saying: "I owe, I owe, so off to work I go!"

Dave: Exactly. I go to work to get paid. When somebody asks you to do work for them, and they have in the back of their mind that as soon as you finish they are not going to pay you, I think that's very bad. Very bad. So what should I do?

Patrick: Particularly when you've got a family to support and other commitments.

Dave: We've got mortgages to pay, the same as they have. If I was to say: "All right then, forget it" and if I got into debt and could not pay my mortgage because of it, nobody is going to come along and say: "Here you are Dave, old chap, here's a few thousand to help you pay the mortgage." Life's not like that. You've got to paddle your own canoe. If you just let them walk all over you, I have found you've got no chance.

The money trap

Patrick: As you very well know, the question of getting paid is the ultimate requisite for staying alive in business, particularly when you're self-employed. When you get paid you're alive in business, which in turn also keeps your private life going. If you don't get paid, it can badly affect both. Don't you agree?

Dave: Absolutely. At the moment there are hundreds of firms going bust because other people won't pay them. They can't get their money in. It's not only people like me who suffer — everyone does.

I've got a friend, he owned a printing firm. He lost his firm. He lost his home. He lost everything he'd owned and worked for, for about 15 years. It's all gone. He's living with his mother now. It's all because people owed him money and wouldn't pay up.

They just said: "We haven't got it. Now you do what you like. It's up to you." And he lost everything.

Just what do you do, in the circumstances?

Patrick: This is particularly the case in the Western world, where you have all these laws to protect both buyer and seller, and you still have the situation where a guy is honest, and does a job with integrity to the satisfaction of the buyer, and the buyer is the person who actually benefits from it — then when the buyer doesn't pay up, the seller finally resorts to the law to recover his money, and only fails further. It is a big tragedy.

Dave: There is nothing nicer than doing a job for somebody, and when you finish they say: "You've made a lovely job of that, Dave. That's lovely. Here's your money." When somebody says to you, "Your work is lovely, we've recommended you to so-and-so and so-and-so", it's a great feeling.

I was in business with my partner, George, for 25 years. We never advertised. All our work came from word of mouth — our customers saying to others: "Dave and George, they're good." That's how we ran our business. We had a few building contractors we worked for, and we stayed in business for 25 years. We had no trouble, except for a few slow payers along the way.

Play safe

Patrick: In pursuing payment, has it ever led to physical assault?

Dave: No. But close. If they see that you're determined, then they back down. They know you're not going to give in and they yield. I also think once they know that you're going to back off from demanding payment, they will take advantage of you.

If you keep the pressure on, it could turn out that they will call the police and blame everything on you and make out that you're the villain.

Patrick: This is the shear deviousness of such people, isn't it? So if you were to give any advice to people who need to get paid for the products or services they are providing, what would it be?

Dave: There is a much better and a less risky way — the way I do it now after learning the hard way.

I wouldn't go to a client and say: "All right, I'll do the job for you. Pay me at the end of the job." I want money (part-payment) as soon as I get the materials, or preferably to buy the materials. Then when I have progressed, say, half-way through the job, I want another draw. Finally, I want the balance on completion.

During that time, at any stage, if you discover they're unable to come up with the money, you won't be so badly off.

Patrick: You mean by getting staggered payments?

Dave: Yes. Even if you get the materials and you get the money for it, you know you've been paid for your materials. You haven't got to fork that out. Your time and so on, you can get over that. But when you've paid out about £300 out of your pocket to the builders' merchant, and you've got to find it, that becomes a more serious thing altogether.

Patrick: O.K. One way out is getting staggered payments. Direct action is the last resort, isn't it?

Dave: Yes, direct action is the last resort.

Patrick: Have you tried to talk them round to paying you? Has it ever worked for you?

Dave: It worked once, but it took a long time. I was aggressive when I went to see him to have a go at him, but he invited me in and we ended-up chatting. He was a genuine man. He didn't have the money. He was honest with me, so I thought, "Well, that's fair enough, let me help this person ride out the situation he's in by not putting too much pressure on him for money which he hasn't got at the moment." He showed me documents relating to the bad financial state he was in, but he said: "As soon as I've got the money, Dave, I'll pay you." And he did.

I had to wait a few months, but I kept my word. He kept his word and paid me. I did another job for him after that, which I got paid for straight away.

Then you will find another man, who'll call you in. He will give you a drink, talk to you sweetly, and then stitch you up.

Patrick: And that, you told me, has happened to you previously in your business life?

Dave: Yes. He's the type who will say: "I'm sorry. I've got no money at the moment. The cheques haven't come in. I'll do this and I'll do that for you." You feel sorry for him. You feel like turning round and giving him a few bob.

You say goodbye to him and he says to you: "Don't worry, I'll definitely have your money in a fortnight's time."

You go back in a fortnight's time and it's the same thing over again. "Oh, I never got paid when I thought I would, and I haven't got this and I haven't got that."

Then you go back again and he gives you another day to come to collect it.

Next time you go back he's not in. His wife

answers the door and says: "Sorry, he's had to go away."
She gives you another night to call round. You go round again and the same thing happens. In the end you get fed up and say to him: "Well, I'm going to wait here for it now, and if you're not going to pay me, I'll have to do something unpleasant about it."

Patrick: Get nasty?

Dave: Yes, if necessary. But then you find that in a couple of days' time he's ringing you. He'll be all nice, telling you he's got your money and you finally go around and collect it.
You shouldn't have to be like that. You shouldn't have to work under those conditions. To me, it is the height of cheek for someone to ask anyone to do work for him knowing he's not wanting to, or not going to, pay. How low can one get? That's terrible. It upsets me. That's all I've got to say on that matter.

Five-point plan

From these real-life examples it can be seen that many sincere, hardworking people, after committing themselves fully to a job of work, and having completed it, have the added trauma of trying to get paid.

In that context it is paramount that the giver must always be prepared to expect the worst and be ready to fight for his money if necessary. In other words, do whatever it takes to get paid. The *modus operandi* is of course dependent on the circumstances, always trying to be legal, decent and fair in your actions.

I know a self-employed businessman who has a very interesting strategy for getting paid. If his payments are not forthcoming, his line of action is as follows:

He sends the debtor

1. A very polite letter requesting payment.

If he gets no response, it is then followed by . . .

2. An abusive phone call.

If he still gets no response, he then writes . . .

3. A threatening letter hinting at legal action and the miseries that could befall the debtor for not paying him.

If he still gets no response, he then makes . . .

4. A further threatening phone call hinting he will take the debtor's right arm as a first instalment, and then the left leg as a second instalment.

If he still gets no response, this will be followed by . . .

5. A summons to court,

by which time it would be sufficient to give the debtor dysentery and he would then **Pay Up!**

Legal steps

A book such as this would never be complete without giving you an overview of some of the legal steps involved in getting paid, when you have failed in your initial efforts.

1. Consider your appropriate legal strategy bearing in mind the enforcement procedure you wish to use after you have obtained judgement.
2. Issue summons in County Court* or a writ in the High Court.
3. You get judgement if the debtor does not respond within 14 days after being served with the court papers. Enforce your judgement by using an appropriate enforcement procedure such as:
   a. issuing a Warrant of Execution requesting the bailiff to attend your debtor's premises to apply for payment or seize sufficient goods to sell by auction if necessary;
   b. applying for a Garnishee Order if monies are owed to your debtor whether by a Bank, Building Society, or any other party;
   c. applying for an Attachment of Earnings Order against individual debtors in regular employment (not limited companies) so that regular deductions from your debtor's wages are made and paid by the employer to the court;
   d. applying for a Charging Order on any interest your debtor has in hand or certain securities he possesses e.g. shares;

* If the debt is £1000 or less, you can make a "small claim" on a do-it-yourself basis through a County Court. There is a helpful series of leaflets on the procedures you need to follow, available from your local County Court. Its address and telephone number are listed in the Telephone Directory under "Courts".

e. applying for an Oral Examination whereby your debtor is ordered to attend court to give evidence of his financial circumstances;
f. bankruptcy proceedings against individual debtors following judgements or after serving Statutory Demands (if the debt is over £750) which may result in Bankruptcy;
g. winding-up proceedings against limited companies (if the debt is over £750) which may result in Liquidation.

If the judgement is placed in the hands of the court bailiffs for enforcement by a Warrant of Execution, this is how I am told they work:

1. The court sends to the debtor an initial warning — Notice of Issue of Warrant of Execution.
2. An initial visit is then made to the debtor's premises to obtain payment. If payment is not received, the bailiff may levy on the debtor's goods to subsequently sell by auction or may take what is known as "Walking Possession" of the debtor's goods.
   "Walking Possession" is a form of agreement made with the debtor authorising the bailiff to re-enter the debtor's premises if the debt is not paid. This gives the debtor an opportunity to pay the debt over a short period of time while the bailiff has technically seized the goods.
3. If payments are defaulted the debtor will receive further action in the form of another visit by the bailiff to remove the goods for sale by auction, or to give the debtor a final opportunity to pay the outstanding amount.
4. If there is no access given to the bailiff, or there are insufficient, or low-value goods (not to justify removal and sale by auction), the bailiff then reports back to the court, who will in turn report back to the creditor stating that they are unable to execute the warrant.
   Note: Don't be put off by this and don't lose heart. You should consider other enforcement options such as a Garnishee Order, Charging Order etc. Your solicitor can advise you on what can be done.

A solicitor's view on debt

This book is a comprehensive guide to collecting the money owed to you. Earlier on we looked at direct action used by some self-employed people and small businesses. We will now look at some of the methods used by larger organisations and experts in the field of debt recovery.

For this purpose I interviewed Tony Sutton, partner and head of the debt recovery department of Tarrant Sutton Solicitors, who has considerable experience in the field of debt recovery. Here is the transcript of our discussion.

Patrick: Hello, Tony. Thank you for giving me your time to be interviewed for **PAY UP!** as both an experienced solicitor and debt collector. Being an expert in pursuing bad debt, can you please elaborate on this subject?

Tony: Yes, indeed. I have been in the business for 14 years and have been involved in practically all areas of debt collection, on anything from TV sets, credit cards and personal loans to commercial and retail work of all descriptions.

Patrick: Once you sell a product, service or idea, what would you say are the main problem areas that one could encounter when it comes to collecting money? After something is sold, I am sure you will agree with me that getting paid can be a completely different ball game. So what are the steps that need to be taken to safeguard your payments?

Tony: Well, obviously, the way that we as a firm look at it is that prevention is better than cure. In other words, a lot of people are more concerned about selling their products or services, and in the excitement and heat of the moment they forget to sort out the very basic requirements such as:

1. Who are you dealing with?
2. What is their name, address and phone number?
3. What terms are you going to be paid on?
4. How much and when?

What I am referring to are the basic details that are obvious when it comes to suing, such as who is going to pay you? For example, you could be dealing with one person, only to find out at the end the day he says that someone else is going to pay — well, then what are you going to do?

To become more legalistic you can ask: "Are they a limited company? An individual, sole trader, or partnership? What is their legal status?"

These are very important criteria when it comes to suing. Any further action you take against an individual or an entity concerned is entirely dependent on their legal status. For example, there are certain things you could do to a limited company which you could not do to an individual. Therefore it is very important that you know whom you are dealing with right from the start.

Patrick: Would you say that people by and large refuse to pay because by nature they are crooks, or is it because they get into financial difficulties in their business, or is it because they don't give too much importance to paying after they have bought something?

Tony: What makes people pay depends on them — it is a very personal thing. In fact, collecting debt becomes a selling exercise in itself which needs to be modified according to the person you are dealing with.

Generally speaking, I believe that most people in this country are honest and want to pay their debts.

Patrick: So where does the dishonest element come in?

Tony: Having said that, the people I deal with are the ones who don't pay their debts and they account for, with some companies, up to 20 per cent of their sales ledger. I would be involved in some sort of legal or collection procedure on behalf of these companies, when they become my client. So you are dealing with certain characteristics of debtors and it is that which I presume you would like me to comment on.

Patrick: Yes, indeed.

Tony: There are two types of debtor. There is the honest fellow, the Mr Nice Guy: you can't get off the telephone because he wants to tell you how badly he is doing, and finding an excuse for not paying and seeking your sympathy. He won't go away from you, and it is in fact very difficult to collect money from someone who is telling you his "I am hard-up" story almost daily.

The other sort of debtor is the one who does not tell you anything about himself. He is quiet throughout the whole of the proceedings you are undertaking and you haven't got a clue why he is not paying up. The important thing is to try and establish during the initial collection procedures what sort of debtor you are dealing with and then adopt and adapt your methods to suit the personality — the psychology — of the person you are trying to collect the money from.

For example, if someone is not telling you anything about what's going on, then it is silly to adopt very expensive procedures with lawyers when you haven't got a clue about who and what you are dealing with. It is better at first to go and take a look for yourself at the debtor's premises, and if you get the chance to interview him, find out what is going on. Why aren't they paying you? Once you establish the reason for the non-payment, then you can set up a strategy which can be "hard" or "soft", whichever way you like to play it.

If people require sympathy and understanding and need time to pay, then you can accordingly formulate a procedure for them to pay up. You do that by setting little tests — hurdles for them to jump over. For example, you can tell them: "O.K., then send me an initial payment. When can you send me the money?" If they say, "I'll send you the money by Tuesday", and if they do, they then pass the test. You then let them pass on to the next stage of the exercise — the next payment. If they fail to honour it, then they fail the test.

Debt collection is all about setting tests for your debtors and letting them clear the hurdle. They either pass or fail it.

The strategy to adopt

Patrick: From what you have told me so far, in the collection procedure there needs to be a well formulated strategy to get the debtor to cough up.

In which circumstance would you use the "soft approach" and when would you use the "heavy artillery"?

Tony: All debts must start off progressively with "soft" collection techniques. To go in extremely hard right at the start could possibly lose you your customer. If you are running a business and you rely on goodwill, then obviously to adopt the "hard" procedures against every debt because it falls overdue would be very short-sighted.

So you must look at your customer and lay out a standard set of procedures for collecting the debt — I am referring to small business here. You set up your monthly/weekly/daily routine necessary to collect your sales ledger. And you would then, say after X days of payment being overdue, make a phone call on this account.

Whether you get through to people or not, you will still send a standard reminder letter requiring payment. If you do not get a response, that should be followed by a second reminder letter and another phone call in (say) a week, two weeks or a month depending on the urgency.

Now in the process of all that action you are going to get people ringing you back and asking you for time to pay and people who are ignoring you. You must therefore deal with each situation on an individual basis. Every debtor's circumstance is different — we are all individual people.

Patrick: Different strokes for different folks!

Tony: Precisely. What makes one debtor pay and another not pay when they have received exactly the same letter is down to the debtor. The debtor who does pay has suddenly reached a stage in the procedures that are being adopted where he does not want to play any more — "That's enough, I'm writing a cheque now because it's getting a bit serious." There are things potentially going to happen which he possibly may not understand and doesn't want to get involved in, so he will pay. If he is in a bad way and hasn't got the money to pay and hasn't contacted you, that is the most difficult case to deal with.

We will continue to adopt standard procedures by going to law — which will cost our client money in paying out for such things as the collection agent's fee, court fees, solicitor's charges, or whatever, in pursuing someone who simply says at the end of the day that they do not have any money.

Patrick: So there are no guarantees in going to law?

Tony: No. In fact we have a couple of sayings here: "There is no point in flogging a dead horse," and "You can't get blood out of a stone!" These adages still apply. At the end of the day, if someone hasn't got any money, then that's it for the time-being, unless you are prepared to wait. If our client is an individual, a sole trader who might have (say) one, two or three debts, it is more likely that he will be prepared to hang on and wait in the hope that he will be paid eventually.

If it is the larger, corporate organisation with a portfolio of bad debts, the less likely they are to wait. As a corporation they make a policy decision to pursue the debt. They cannot have all those bad debts hanging on to the end of their sales ledger with their solicitor doing nothing about it. When the solicitor says "Hold on, we've got a judgement", and that means by law they have up to six years to pursue the debt, they are not interested in that. They have to write off the debt and forecast their bad debts for the following year. So they have to make provisions in their accounts for bad debts — in reality they will write off debts if they are not successful in collecting them within a reasonable time.

That's the way it goes. At the end of the day as far as debtors are concerned we have another saying we apply: "Persistence beats resistance!" This means if you keep persisting, eventually you may hit upon something that the debtor has either never experienced before, or doesn't want to go through with, and that would make him pay. By being persistent you are attempting to change his behaviour towards the debt.

The hard line

Patrick: So far, I gather, you have been talking in general about the "soft approach". What would your "hard approach" be like?

Tony: The "hard approach" is adopting a less understanding position. To do that you must separate yourself from the debtor. You have tried the "soft approach", but it has not worked. So you adopt a much colder, less involved approach and you take a harder line. You basically say, "Pay up or else . . ."

Patrick: Is this done by phone, or letter, or both?

Tony: It would be done by a combination of both. If he does not pay up you should adopt any legitimate procedure available to you to get a response of some sort.

Patrick: Could you please give me a summary of what the "hard approach" would be?

Tony: Well, the way the law operates in this country, as you probably know, having researched it, is that over a £750 debt you can bring insolvency proceedings, which unfortunately is expensive. But for larger debts there is absolutely no doubt that the insolvency approach, such as Statutory Demands under the Insolvency Act 1986 followed by Bankruptcy Petitions or Winding-Up Petitions, is a very effective route to collecting debts. And certainly when I first started practising, bankruptcy and winding-up proceedings were something very few people knew about and got involved with.

Nowadays, particularly in the field of debt recovery, they are much more common procedures. The lawyer would recommend the client adopts this action for two or three very good reasons. One is that a debtor could have other County Court summonses, other High Court writs, and many other letters and telephone calls from collection agencies or solicitors at a given time, which does not give you an advantage.

So when he gets his post in the morning, he will look at it and prioritise his mail — for example, "That's a County Court summons, I don't need to worry about that for 14 days. That's a High Court writ, I don't need to do anything for 21 days. That's a Statutory Demand, I've got 21 days to deal with that. That's a seven-day letter from a collection agency, nothing is going to happen on that because they will go away and write me another one."

They become familiar with these techniques. However, at any one time there can only be one Bankruptcy Petition or one Winding-Up Petition for an individual or limited company. So if a debtor receives one of those, then that is the first thing that is going to be looked at. We do a letter called a seven-day winding-up letter, which threatens to wind-up a company if it does not pay its debts in seven days on the grounds that it is insolvent and unable to pay its debts as they fall due. There is a provision in the Insolvency Act which says that one of the grounds for winding-up or presenting a Winding-Up Petition against a company is on the basis that it is unable to pay its debts as they fall due — that is a seven-day letter — you could do it on a four-day letter or however many days you wish to give them. It is becoming commonplace nowadays to use this sort of letter as part of the collection strategy. Even if at the end of the day the creditor decides not to issue a petition, simply to send a letter makes the company receiving it wake up.

The psychological approach

Patrick: Now I can see the difference between the "soft" and "hard" approaches. But in the final analysis, whatever approach you use must achieve the objective of getting the debtor to **Pay Up!** And it must be used with wisdom, because the way I look at it is that the debtor is another person like one of us, and therefore we have to manage the situation with a certain amount of feeling for others. To use a sledge hammer to crack a nut, it doesn't serve the purpose.

Now, going back to the earlier part of our discussion, you referred to the honest and talkative debtor who gives you loads of sob-stories and you have to hassle to get money from this guy. Then you referred to the silent debtor who is difficult to get to grips with and therefore necessitates some groundwork to be done by, say, visiting him and possibly interviewing him, before you decide whether to go in "soft" or "hard". Are there any other categories?

Tony: Let me clarify that further. You have the talkative honest, talkative dishonest, silent honest and silent dishonest. The difficult ones are always the quiet ones, because you never know whether you are dealing with a debtor who has a genuine problem that needs to be sorted out and scheduled into some sort of repayment plan or a package that works. Or, whether they do have the money, but they are keeping their heads down and they are dishonest and they in fact don't intend to pay you. They will wait as long as possible without paying because that is their strategy of keeping you waiting to see whether you will give up because of the time lapse and cost. There are lots of businesses and companies that fall into this category.

There are certain businesses, particularly in the self-employed field, who are more vulnerable — such as graphic artists and photographers who do work for people or companies — and they are lucky if they get paid. They dare not chase for the money (a) because of the cost involved, (b) because the debtor's policy may only be to pay when really forced to do so, and they do not want to go through all the hassle or (c) because they believe that if they did push for the money they are not likely to get any further work.

Patrick: And it is a great shame that some self-employed businesspeople are used by some of these large corporations to get work done and then don't get paid by them. But the problem with some of these self-employed individuals is that they do not have the muscle to take on the big boys. If only they had the front to pursue their debtors through the law, they stand a better chance of getting their money than a big company trying to get money from an individual. And in fact that did happen to me.

A big corporation owed me money in sales commission which they did not pay. After they'd turned a blind eye to repeated requests for settlement, I took them to court and got judgement against them. I sent in the bailiffs and they paid up. Then, on the other hand, I dealt with a self-employed businessman who did me for £2,600 and I lost that money and more, even though I got judgement against him and sent in the bailiffs twice.

Tony: You could bet your bottom dollar — with big companies heads will roll if they find themselves receiving a County Court summons. The senior management would want to know why they received the summons and who is responsible for it. Certainly this is our conclusion from several years' experience. The large companies aren't in fact the problem.

The biggest problems come from people who have small businesses — trading names where creditors do not know who they are dealing with. And as I said right from the start, it is very important to identify the very basic criteria of what's involved, who you are dealing with, what is their legal status, when you will be paid or who is going to pay you. It seems silly even to ask those questions, but they are really very important to getting your money through the legal channels. People buy things because they *want* to buy them. And it is not difficult to introduce something right from the start, such as "When are you going to pay me for all this?" — and so on.

Patrick: It seems to be a British disease where people

are so reluctant to ask details about the money they are working for. They just do not have the nerve to bring out the question of payment and they lose out as a consequence. They would rather go back and curse the buyer, saying that he was a bad guy, instead of coming out straight and saying, "Can I have my cheque please?" Getting paid could be as simple as that.

Tony: It requires simple point-of-sale stuff. In the law now, when we take on new clients we are required to tell them what we are going to charge them, because historically speaking no one knew what they were going to be billed for until the end of the case. This previously put people off going to law to collect debts and things like that. So now there is a body of solicitors that have emerged who are highly experienced in the field of debt recovery. We, for example, negotiate with clients on a fairly large scale in terms of what fee structure there would be for the collection of their debts. That generally is reviewed annually with the clients. These are very important things. We ourselves get bad debts sometimes. Usually they are caused simply by the client not fully understanding what he is getting into, and how much it is going to cost him. Another cause is that some businesses, particularly the corporate ones, are going bust these days.

Anyway, coming back to the different type of debtor we were talking about: as I have already told you, the quiet ones are the most difficult because you can spend a lot of money, only to find out in some cases that they have no money and you really have been flogging a dead horse. And you should just give up, call it a day, realise when you are beaten — that is the best commercial decision to make.

The noisy ones are easy enough because you can set those tests or hurdles which become a very important part of the strategy. Being prompt on these hurdles is also important. If he says he is ringing you on Tuesday and doesn't, then you remind *yourself* to ring him on Tuesday.

Another thing you should do is to look at your procedures and ask yourself, for example, "Why did that happen? Why did we allow it to occur? What went wrong?" and you put controls in so that any shortcomings will be rectified or minimised in the future. That could be credit vetting — you set low credit authorisation levels so that, say, anybody could get credit up to £200, but above that limit everybody is credit-checked. You will obviously set your limit depending on the goods or services that you are selling and the type of people you are dealing with. You suggest that larger companies may be bad paymasters — well, yes, they can sit on their money for as long as possible — they juggle with the cash so that the smaller creditors will be kept at bay for longer and some may give up and not bother chasing their debts.

We have computer systems here that provide a diary ahead — they monitor cases, check them out and churn out standard letters to chase up debtors who default. The systems here most of the time are applying the court system for chasing debtors, although there are letter cycles that we run for various clients.

The direct approach

Patrick: Now for the purpose of this book I have interviewed some small businessmen who had bad-debt problems. They by-passed the legal profession as they did not have too much faith in it and took direct action to recover their money. They used a combination of heavy-handed verbal and physical action, not actual assault but something very near to it — close to the bone! What are your feelings about that kind of approach? What I am trying to accomplish through this book is to give readers an array of tactics and techniques which they can fearlessly use with discretion, obviously without any recourse to physical violence, and within the framework of the law, to enable them to get paid. Hence I have listed the varied selection of examples told to me.

Tony: The legal procedures are simply one of a number of different strategies available to people. It is not necessarily the right way. If, say, a debtor is thick-skinned and has experienced a lot of legal proceedings in his time he gets resistant to it. He can survive. He knows that nothing can happen — it doesn't matter.

Going on to direct action, in its own way it is right. I wouldn't advocate physical violence in any way. There are a lot of people who will visit the debtor directly or instruct collectors to call in person — door-knockers — to collect the debt.

Patrick: The way I see it is that there is this aspect of righteousness involved. From the creditor's (seller's) angle it has cost him in time, money and labour to offer his product, service or idea to the buyer (debtor). The buyer uses it, and in return what he is required to do is to pay for what he has had; if he doesn't pay up, what it really means is that (a) he is ridiculing the creditor and (b) he is affecting both his business and private life because that income is his lifeblood. Therefore I see it as a legitimate reason for the creditor to take that sort of action.

Tony: There is a very strong moral code in the creditor's camp and we are part of that. We sincerely want to collect debts. Collecting a debt for us is good news. And that is felt all the way along the line and it starts with the client. The more enthusiasm the client shows towards the task, the more energetic we become. The less interested the client is, the less inclined are we. Therefore, commenting on the direct approach, yes — there is a very strong moral reason to take it when you have been ripped off by someone after you have done a good job and he has not paid you. There is a sense of total frustration after you have spent all that time to give all those resources to no avail at all — you get nowhere! So a visit to the debtor certainly is not a bad thing, providing you can handle it sensibly, within the framework of the law, and you are prepared to accept the possible consequences of what may occur.

You may have not met your debtor before. When you turn up on his doorstep you may discover that he is a six-and-a-half-foot giant and he's surrounded by Dobermann guard dogs — you never know what you could come across. So you must always go accompanied, so that you have a witness to what takes place and possibly for your own protection. You may find that your debtor is living in the middle of a field and is looking after cows — you never can tell until you go there. So direct action does have its place in debt recovery. One of the problems if it fails is that the creditor's sense of frustration will be even greater and really there is not a lot more left you can do except go to law and hope for the best.

PAYMENT IN KIND

A council bailiff, hired to collect bad debts on rents, had one debtor who never paid up. He went around to her flat time and time again, but never took the money, and the council never received their rent. But the bailiff was never unhappy about the situation and used to go back week after week — but still there was no change.

In the end a council investigation revealed why they never received the money for the flat and yet the woman was still their tenant. It transpired that the debtor was giving the bailiff payment of a different kind.

Patrick: What are your feelings towards bartering? If, say, the debtor tells the creditor, "I cannot pay you in cash but you can take two of my cows."

Tony: That's fine, if the creditor is prepared to accept it. You may even want to take back some of your products and credit him for what you take back. He may even have some other goods that you may want to buy off him. That's fine, as long as you cover it in your accounting books the correct way.

In your research you may have heard about R.O.T. clauses — "Retention of Title" clauses — where creditors, if they haven't been paid, can go in and collect their goods. And that again is a preventative measure that is taken at the point-of-sale.

A repayment programme which initially could be on the small side, will at least train the debtor to make regular payments. This feeling of reluctance to pay you, either because he hasn't got any money and therefore can't, or because he doesn't want to, is something which must be broken. The way you can do that is by creating a regular pattern in his mind that every month he is going to pay you something.

Some interesting cases

Patrick: Debt recovery is a management problem, isn't it?

Tony: Exactly.

Patrick: With all your experience, Tony, as a practising lawyer involved in the field of debt recovery, there may be some interesting stories for you to tell which have happened over the last 15 years.

Tony: Sure. Without mentioning names, some of them relate more to the procedures we have adopted. But they do demonstrate what can happen. There was the case of a bank that had not paid its minicab fares to a minicab company with which they held an account. So we sued the bank concerned. Being a bank, of course, you would have expected them to have loads of money.

Patrick: Was that bank *bankrupt?*

Tony: No, but we thought it was a good basis to sue on behalf of the minicab firm. The bank failed to respond to the County Court summons. We got judgement and sent in the bailiffs to the head office, whereupon the company secretary rang me up. We had a bit of a barney about it because he was wondering what on earth I was doing suing his bank. I told him it was because they hadn't paid their debt. He then tried to point out to me that being a bank there would be no problem. I said that quite clearly there had been a problem, otherwise we would not be in this position today. To cut a long story short, I guess it must have been the best day the bailiffs ever had — going into a bank to collect money. It was not even a large amount of money, about £300 or £400. But it was enough to get to the top, for the company secretary to ring me and criticise the procedures we adopted to cover up their embarrassment at their company not paying their debt. That was his only way out. It ended by him paying up.

Talking about large companies not paying their debts, I can remember a fairly big manufacturer of machine equipment, who received a County Court summons we issued on behalf of our client. It was again not a big amount and it was passed on to their legal department. A solicitor from their legal department rang me to say that they accepted the fact that they owed the money and that they were sending us a cheque for the debt. I pointed out to the solicitor that there was a liability for the payment of the interest and the cost of the proceedings, to which he told me that it was their company policy not to pay any costs and interest when they were being sued and that if my client wanted to do any more business with them again then he'd better withdraw the claim for interest and costs. I then asked the solicitor whether he had been to law school and he confirmed to me he had. Then I asked him if he knew the "Green Book" — the practitioner's guide to County Court procedure. He said he did. In that case, I told him, I did not understand why his company thought they were above the law — to which he replied that my client could either take it or leave it. The nett effect of that was that we proceeded with the summons, got the judgement and put the bailiffs in just for the costs and interest, which was not really a lot of money but more a matter of principle. And that was paid. And that again was a clear example of a major corporation not paying its debts and creating an internal policy which was against the law. I felt it was outrageous of them to behave in that way, because that was not what we expected from captains of industry.

Patrick: You mentioned to me the story of a crane.

Tony: Yes. It was a debtor company. It owed quite a substantial debt. And the only real asset it had was an enormous crane. It was so big that when it came to enforcing the judgement, the sheriff's officers had to book all the people on the site for a week to take the crane apart and remove it to be sold. In the process of all that going on, the worried debtor managed to find some money to stop the action as his major

asset was being dismantled in front of him. Now let me tell you another one. I am sure you may have heard of "garnishee". You can garnishee either bank or building society accounts.

Patrick: Can you explain the garnishee order in a bit more detail?

Tony: Yes. Well, I guess the bank account is the easiest to describe. If your debtor has a bank account which is in credit and has money in it, then you can make an application to the court after you have obtained the judgement for an order that the money that is in credit in the debtor's bank account be paid to you from the bank.

And the money is frozen in the bank to satisfy the judgement — the court can do that. This is an extremely effective remedy. It also has an even better effect where it can be applied to a third party who owes money to your

debtor. So, in other words, if one of your debtor's debtors hasn't paid him, you can obtain an order from the court (after a judgement) that your debtor's debtor pays you directly instead of your debtor.

This leads me on to my next story, which involved a company that was owed money for hire of some plant. The debtor was a self-employed truck driver who delivered aggregate in a dump truck. He used to work on a site where he filled up his truck and went and emptied it somewhere else. My client told me that was all he knew about what their debtor was doing, and asked me whether we could do anything for him regarding it. We worked out that that the truck driver was paid by the number of loads he carried. So every fortnight we served a garnishee on the company paying him. We served the garnishee order three times. On each of the three occasions the order was served on a Thursday. But when he went on a Friday to collect his wages, his employer told him: "Sorry, we can't pay you the money as we have to pay it on this order we have received." And he was so fed up, he rang us up and told us what he thought of us. But he continued working and eventually after three occasions over six weeks he paid the debt off. That was very successful.

Here is another example involving garnishee. A private client had a judgement over a debtor. He tried many ways to get payment from this chap but failed. Although the debtor had a limited company he traded from a flat. He was a builder. The creditor waited for nearly two years, but in all that time the plan was to wait for the moment to establish where the debtor was working. And eventually he did stumble across it. He reported the details to us and we were able to obtain a garnishee order so that the people at the site at which the debtor was working paid us.

The business of debt collection

Patrick: You seem to have an impressive track record in debt recovery. How do you find it as a job?

Tony: I love it. We get a terrific buzz out of it in terms of pursuing the debtor and collecting the money. Don't misunderstand me — there is no vindictive streak to it. We just feel that we are on the side of right and are sorry when clients aren't able to collect the money. We are terribly enthusiastic about it, providing (as I told you earlier) the client has also a "go for it" attitude.

If on the other hand all the client wants to do is tell us, for example, "Don't tell me about it, I really don't want to know anything and I am not really interested about what's possible . . ." it won't motivate us sufficiently. What we would like to see is clients enthusiastically asking us what we could do for them, and there is a heck of a lot we could do and would do on their behalf.

Patrick: I would like to butt in and ask you something. We know that there are all these safeguards in law, but in the final analysis there comes a point, if you take it to its extreme, where the possible outcome is making someone bankrupt or putting a company into liquidation. In other words, the medicine could be so strong that it becomes worse than the disease. How do you reconcile yourself with the moral dilemma where you put a small businessman out of business which was his livelihood. Now this guy had difficulty in paying your client because others were not paying him, and you start hunting him — that doesn't seem fair.

Tony: We are charged with the responsibility of pursuing the debt on behalf of our client. In the procedures we adopt we don't want to unnecessarily make people bankrupt or wind them up. However, that can be an inevitable consequence of the actions we take. And when we do those things it is important that the client understands that it can occur. Some of the clients positively want that to happen. They see it as a means of hitting back — "He's not paid me, so I want to see him bankrupt." They feel very strongly about it. I think that if you are in business you have to adopt a business head to these matters. To get too personally involved can almost destroy your clear-sightedness and your ability to get paid. In fact, the more emotional a creditor becomes, the more difficult the task of debt collection gets because you are putting too much of yourself into it.

Collection is more like selling, in a way. The debtor is on the phone and you are talking to him. You are selling an idea to him. The potential consequences of him not paying you could be to his disadvantage. You are trying to get him to take a specific action and it is a balance between how far you push it and how far you don't. And you measure the response as the debtor talks to you. The classic thing we now get is: "I haven't got any money, and if you make me bankrupt you are not going to get paid and neither is anyone else." And that is the standard reply we find more and more people give.

The answer to that is "O.K., what can we do about it? Let's see if we can find a suitable answer to the problem — you didn't have to ring me up to tell me to take whatever action we might want to take. You obviously felt that it was important enough to ring me, and I am pleased about that. This matter obviously is of importance to my client or else it would not have been passed on to us. When you entered into a contract with our client, don't tell me that you never intended to pay him for the products or services you took. Of course you did. In that case we should be working together towards sorting something out, rather than you telling me now that you haven't got any money to pay." Now the more the debtor reacts personally or aggressively to either me or my staff, the more involved we become. We are pro-active — a lot of people think solicitors are reactive, but we are a pro-active firm. We have a department here that does telephone-chasing and letter-writing. Its job is to try and shake the money out before using the legal processes. Why do people think that all lawyers do is write letters? — our staff in fact are very competent on the phone, as we are meant to be. Our professional training and approach is reflected in our ability to communicate and our desire to do so. The legal process is usually the last resort. Some clients want to go in by taking a hard line immediately, and that we do. We advise them in advance about the pros and cons of their strategy.

The unpredictable debtor

Patrick: Now there are a lot of things you can do at your end. But looking at it from the debtor's side, all your actions and those of his other creditors can culminate possibly in severe stress for him. With multiple debts and so many people breathing down his neck, how would he portray anxiety to you?

Tony: He can be very aggressive — abusive. We have loads of that regularly; it's not a problem to us — we have been conditioned to it. We believe sincerely that the creditor is always right — he has instructed us and we are acting for him in his best interest. There are a couple more stories I would like to tell you. Here is the story of the dead debtor.

We were pursuing a small debt. We had a phone call from someone who said he was a relative of the debtor and that he had died. And that was it! We made what inquiries we could but couldn't establish that he had died.

Anyway, lo and behold, some time later a man walked into reception and said his name was Mr Smith or whatever, and he had the letter that we originally wrote to him. Some of the people in the litigation department nearly had a heart attack. "Mr Smith, Mr Smith, you're alive, you're alive!" they shouted. He had risen from the dead and come back to pay his debts! We were all delighted that he had managed to do that just for that day! It just shows you they don't all do what others say they have done!

Patrick: What about the case of the two fighting brothers?

Tony: That's a good one. Two Greek brothers were fighting amongst themselves because one

owed money to the other. We represented the brother who was owed the money and it was all disputed and there was a lot of trouble brewing. They did not speak to each other for months while all this was going on. I needed some instructions by phone from the one we were acting for, and he went all quiet. I bumped into him later and asked him what was going on. He said everything was now O.K. and that he did not want me to do any more work on the matter. He said he met his brother and that they were now good friends again. I asked him what happened? He said he was in a pub and that he got into a fight. And he said that as the fight was going on he realised that someone was fighting on his side and he discovered it was his brother. And after the fight was over they made up with each other. And I suppose that is another way of getting rid of a debt.

Detective work

Tony: I have another one to tell you. The client was a wholesaler of electrical equipment, and the debtor was a self-employed electrical contractor. He had goods on credit which he hadn't paid for and had been through the legal procedures with us, but we failed to collect any money at all and the case had been a complete disaster. The client rang me up and asked me what we should do, and I asked him whether he had any other information on the chap. He said no, but he would see if he could find out something new. Then he rang me back a few weeks later to say that the debtor had been overheard boasting in a local shop that he had a motor cruiser that he kept in Poole harbour.

We then told our client to find out more details about it — such as its name, its colour and so on — which he was able to do. We issued a writ to enable us to seize the boat in Poole harbour. And the debt was paid pretty quickly after that.

So what it goes to show is that in a lot of these cases a little relevant knowledge is not a bad thing! Knowing your debtor's habits, knowing more about his lifestyle, knowing people who know him and can tell you about him — fact-finding done on your own does help a lot. You can by all means pay investigators to find out information — private detectives for instance.

Patrick: Do some of your clients use private detectives?

Tony: Oh, yes. Private detectives can be very useful. Collecting debts is all about finding information, and as you probably gathered it could be luck. It just could happen that you were in the right place at the right time. That's it. The information needed is found out and the debt gets paid. It can also be the opposite, where you get everything you want to know but you don't get paid.

Patrick: The other thing, Tony — the United Kingdom is a civilised country where most people operate within the framework of the law. If, say, you were in the U.S.A., do they use similar strategies to ours over here, or would techniques be more heavy-handed? The Mafia, for example — if you owe them money, they would I guess first rearrange your face and then fill you up with a round of lead bullets, then shrug their shoulders and say, "That's business!"

Tony: I guess that's another way of solving the debt problem — the final solution!

I understand in America they are more

aggressive and more attorney-conscious. Most businesses over there don't go into business unless they have been to their attorney and drafted up some sort of formal agreement with each other that sets out the basis on which they are going to trade. That means when it comes to litigation they run straight to the lawyers and blame them for drawing up the agreement that doesn't enable them to get paid. Another thing they do over there is that attorneys in debt collection are paid on a commission basis on successful collection — what we call a contingency-fee basis, which in England is not allowed for litigation. The lawyers may employ part-time students to go and do some initial investigative work on behalf of the creditor, to find out what the debt is all about. They report back to the lawyer and say that this man or company is worth suing. And based on that, the lawyer will say: "O.K., I'll take this case on. My commission on this case if I succeed will be X per cent but I do not want the other three debts to handle." What the creditor does on those remaining cases I do not know. But as far as the law is concerned, they are much more litigation-conscious. In some European countries, I am told, you have statutory interest of delay for non-payment. In the northern parts of Europe in particular, any creditor is able to charge their debtors interest on any unpaid invoices. I fully endorse that. It is outrageous that people should not be entitled to charge or be charged interest for late payment.

Patrick: And I am also told that the law is more stringent on the Continent with regard to debt recovery — if you default, you go straight to court.

Tony: Yes. And another thing is that they have a lot

of trade journals where they publish the list of bad payers. The local community Chambers of Commerce have a high standing and they too keep lists of defaulters. So if you buy a trade magazine they report who is suing whom. These are all terribly important, to get people more aware of what's going on. I have always advocated that one of the biggest problems in small business is that you need to know business names. We call them "firms" in the law. It is basically a trading style under which either a limited company or two individuals or a sole proprietor can trade. Well, when you walk down the high street, you look at a shop, it says "SMELLY'S BOUTIQUE" on the outside and you haven't got a clue whom you are dealing with. You go in there and you sell them something or you repair their boiler or whatever, and you invoice "SMELLY'S BOUTIQUE" and they don't pay you — they owe you £150 or £200. You have no idea of whom you dealt with, and you have a big problem on your hands.

Now I think that there should be a local government department charged with the responsibility of finding out who owns what in the locality and publicising it, so that anyone dealing with any of these businesses can go and search to find out who it is.

Patrick: That could tantamount to fraud in the "SMELLY'S BOUTIQUE" case, couldn't it?

Tony: That is a sweeping statement to make. Fraud would mean that they never intended to pay you. It is very difficult to prove. If the creditor never asks whom they are dealing with, it couldn't be misconstrued as fraudulent. Who is to blame in that case? The seller in that situation is the author of his own misfortune because he has not taken the trouble to find out whom he is dealing with right from the outset.

So, going back to trade journals and so on, bad publicity is not good for debtors but it is a good thing for creditors. For example, in the trade journal of electrical services, if it said "Whatever you do, don't deal with these companies because they have been blacklisted for non-payment" then you are forewarned.

Patrick: It does not automatically follow, just because a person does not pay one creditor, that he is not going to pay others. He could be selective and pick and choose. So here again, if you analyse it, there are no hard-and-fast rules. Life is not made up of certainties or guarantees.

Tony: Correct. You must mix and match all your procedures and collection techniques to suit the debtor concerned. To simply adopt a standard set of procedures (unless you are a very large organisation with very similar accounts) wouldn't necessarily be practical, you could do what is called a "debtor profile". For example, this could show that our average debtor is say a small trader, he has an overdraft of £5,000 with his bank, his competitors are so-and-so, he doesn't have a new car . . . In other words, build a profile of him.

Patrick: Could you say, for example, that this is a good risk . . . and that is a bad one?

Tony: Yes — we have particular types of debtor who are a higher risk than others. For example, in the industry we would consider that advertising debts, and debts based on services provided, are more difficult to collect. Debts involving opinion based on the quality of artistic work provided, for example photography, architecture — your customer may say, "The work you did was lousy, I didn't like it" — you could get into difficult corners with stuff like that. It produces the spurious or phoney defence — a lot of debtors put up defences or dispute claims simply to buy time. It is therefore very important, going back to basics, that you adopt procedures, so that if you can get hold of your debtor and get him to either admit that he owes you the money or tell you when he is going to pay you, then you should record that either by confirming it to him in writing or by entering it in an internal log. If it is a telephone log, record the date, whom you spoke to, the comments, and your conclusions. This you can then put before the court at an early stage and say, "Look, this chap is taking the mickey!" If you don't do all of that and he says "I dispute it", then you have the record to prove your side of it.

The legal penalties

Patrick: Can you go to jail if you owe people money?

Tony: Not for non-payment of debt. But you can be imprisoned for contempt of court for failing to turn up for certain types of hearing.

In the oral examination procedure in the County Court, if the debtor fails to attend the second hearing it can lead to imprisonment. An oral examination is where you apply to court for an order, ordering the debtor to attend the court on a certain date to give evidence as to his means. The purpose of the exercise is entirely exploratory and is intended to ask him a series of questions about his financial affairs. He goes on oath and has to swear that everything he says is the truth and it is all written down. You can then look at the financial questionnaire that he provides answers to and decide what you wish to do. Then there is another procedure, called the "Attachment of Earnings". In this you make an application to the court for an order for a certain amount of money, which in fact is means-tested, to be deducted from his wages and paid by his employers to the court.

The difficulties with both of those procedures are that, in the case of the oral examination, the debtor rarely turns up at the first hearing, and the shear cost of going to court is quite high. The debtor may be imprisoned for contempt of court if he doesn't turn up on a subsequent hearing. The only way out for the debtor if he fails to turn up is to tell the court: "I am sorry I did not turn up for the last hearing; here is all the information about my financial situation."

In the case of the Attachment of Earnings, if the debtor is an individual and not a company and fails to complete a County Court form as to the circumstances regarding his employment so that regular deductions are made by the employer and forwarded to the court, it could have the same consequences as for oral examination.

Generally speaking, people are not sent to prison for non-payment of a debt unless it is a criminal offence and that is fraud. You have to show that at the time the debtor ordered your goods or services he had no intention of paying you. That is a very difficult thing to prove because any creditor with any sense certainly wouldn't be supplying a debtor or potential debtor with goods or services if he knew he wasn't going to get paid.

Patrick: That brings me to a very important point. How is it that a limited company can more or less be released from their liability, but a sole proprietor is liable for all his debts?

Tony: Well, that's the law! A limited company really is a vehicle under which the law allows groups of people to trade collectively as one business. This business has a separate limited legal identity which is quite distinct from the individual people who run it. If that legal entity incurs debts, it does so on its own behalf and is responsible in law for its own demise. Sole proprietors, on the other hand, are in themselves legal entities who if they incur debts are personally responsible for them.

I think we are looking here more at the smaller business or smaller limited company that is in effect nothing more than the limited-company-equivalent of sole traders or sole proprietors. That's where the problem really lies — it is that area of the small company that maybe consists of one or two people. It may even be a consultant engineer who does self-employed work for people, but has a limited company.

The reason they have protection is because they are limited by the value of the company, which is limited by share-holding. You can have limited partnerships whereby some of the partners are limited to their liability, but others aren't. I think really that the days are getting short for the small limited company that has the protection that it does, because you can close them down and start them up as you see fit. Very often you have limited company "XYZ SALES LTD" going down and all of a sudden you have "XYZ HOLDINGS" in its place. The same people are running the same show. That happens very often in this country. It is morally wrong. As far as the law is concerned at the moment — I didn't write the law! But certainly the intention of the Cork Report before the Insolvency Act was passed was to make directors of limited companies more accountable for their actions. However, what has really occurred is that only if they are grossly fraudulent and trade very badly could they be personally liable. But even then their liability by law is only to the extent to which the company has suffered a loss as a result of their wrongful activities. So the loss which has got to be paid for by the director is the loss suffered by the company and is paid to the company in liquidation; it is not paid to the creditors. It may be for the benefit of the creditors. The chances are that the director of a small company has given personal guarantees, the company has gone down and if he is sued there is no money — he has got no money. So a lot of insolvency practitioners dealing in liquidations simply don't have the resources, or the directors that they wish to pursue don't have the available funds to make it worthwhile pursuing them. Prevention is better than cure, as it is always. But in the case of the sole traders, they can be made personally bankrupt. But as it is frequently being pointed out to us by debtors, they can apply for a discharge in two years' time.

So, if, say, you are a self-employed sole proprietor (and I should not be telling people how not to pay their debts) and you are made bankrupt, and two years later your spouse wished to run a business and you simply were to manage it, then your spouse or an associate could incur new credit on your behalf, on the basis that you are effectively managing the business. Looking at it from a legal angle, you would be simply running the shop and not in charge of it. You could still be running a business through third parties for that two-year period until you apply for the discharge. So in effect the problem is not completely solved, even if someone goes bankrupt. But we all believe that people are basically honest. We can only take measures to reduce our losses at the end of the day, on the basis that prevention is better than cure! That approach is much better, after all.

Patrick: You have given me some humorous stories. Do you have any frightening ones?

Tony: Not really, and we should never be frightened. However there is one unusual case that comes to my mind. We presented a Winding-Up Petition to a company and were proceeding against it on behalf of a client of ours because it owed him money for work provided. All the company really was offering was an idea. It was in the process of selling the idea — intellectual property — to one of the public utility concerns. We were effectively asked to back off, otherwise this company felt we could possibly blow out the whole deal for them because of our legal foothold. The debtor felt that nobody would have been interested in dealing with it because of the legal implications. What happened was that the company came to us and made us believe that it was worthwhile our stepping back because the idea was so good and that it was going to go ahead and get it converted into cash.

The idea these people had in mind was a marketing one. They somehow paid us and we backed off. It was a success. And that idea I now see everwhere I go. Only *I* know that idea was saved from insolvency at the eleventh hour. That was good. The debtor stood up, came forward, and sold the idea to us, and we convinced our client that it was the right thing to do. So that is really a case of a debtor fighting for survival and our client got noticed because he had taken action. Had it been just an ordinary summons, letter or telephone call, it would probably have been ignored. But because our client was going for the "jugular vein" — the hardest line — he was noticed.

The art of credit management

Patrick: Now let's look at this whole aspect of debt recovery and try to give it some depth and meaning: we as individuals work and offer our goods, services or ideas for sale. People buy them, and they either pay or they don't. If they don't pay you, the one who is selling has major problems because he needs that income to keep his business and family alive. Success in fact is measured by money coming in and the profit being earned to maintain that lifestyle. In a nutshell, the matter of paying up is a very simple thing. All it takes is the signing of a cheque or paying cash. Under this simple act is a minefield of legal complexities, stress and strife. Can it be avoided?

Tony: That is right. It can be really horrifying. The cost that people can get into in terms of a simple debt that is owed to them is perplexing if they get involved with lawyers and adopt many different legal procedures. Therefore, to save you the headache of all this it is so important to get things right from the start. Or to put it another way, "the good sale is the one that brings in the cheque or the cash". In the early days when I was involved in debt recovery, if I went out and met someone and they asked me, "What do you do?" and I replied, "I am a solicitor invloved in debt collection", they wouldn't even like to talk to me. But now it is a case of credit management — the art of risk management — assessing whether the debt is going to be bad or not before you even give them the products or services — also, monitoring the account while you are providing it to them — chasing the debt when it is not paid — using all the support services that are attached to the collection cycle, applying the legal procedures when necessary and using the investigation process when necessary, and all that. That is now recognised as an industry that is absolutely essential to cash flow management in most major corporations.

There are many businesses competing for a share of this market. You can:

1. factor your debts by selling them to a factoring company who will then go and chase your debts;
2. take out credit insurance — by paying a single premium per annum you can then avail yourself of a collection service and litigation if required;
3. employ private investigators, personal and telephone collection agents and solicitors;
4. use invoice discounting.

Alternatively you can knock on the door yourself if you choose to. But how you do it is what counts. And it is something you have got to be aware of, that it is all there at the point-of-sale, and ask yourself, "What are the basic things that I have got to look at? Why am I doing this? What am I trying to achieve?"

A logical answer to that would be, "I am here because it is my living." There is no point issuing invoices that never get paid. You have got to realise that right at the start your sole objective must be to get paid. It is interesting to note what you said earlier on, that people do work hard and offer their products or services for sale and then hope that they are going to get paid, never discussing the most important thing — "Why are we doing this?" — the answer being, "to get paid." So that is how this issue must be tackled. For example, chasing a debt by telephone you could say: "When are you going to send me my cheque?" — "Could you tell me, when can the cheque be ready to be picked up?" — "Could you please give me the number of the cheque?"

Basically, this is your living. By increasing the collection of information right from the start, it means that all of these other things that you may need to do at the end can be narrowed down. You can choose the right course. You will be better off than a lot of people playing the guessing game and asking themselves when they are confronted with the problem of bad debt, "Now what should I do?" For example, in law they could issue a summons or a writ. Then they ask, "Now what should I do next?" You tell them to get a judgement and send the bailiffs in. In my view that is not exciting work. That is a sausage-machine approach, very mechanical and does not guarantee your money. It is not pro-active debt collection. Don't get me wrong, that needs to be done. But on top of all of that you need to say, "But ah, I found out this bit of information, I found out that." It is like doing a little detective work before you apply the medicine.

If you have to sue people when they haven't paid you, that shouldn't worry you. What you should be concerned about is spending a fortune on legal services simply to achieve no result. You should therefore really look at the target and say, "What am I aiming for?" It is not just the money that you should be concerned with — you should ask yourself, "What option should I take in all these things I have at my disposal?" and then discuss the strategy so that you do not go and waste your money on all these routes to end up actually exhausted, having accomplished nothing.

From the outset, the more friendly you are with your debtor, the more information you are able to glean about his habits, for example, where he hangs about and so on, the better your chances are.

Patrick: There is a big problem I feel that exists. When you are trying to sell to them you have to be friendly and let a cordial atmosphere prevail as much as possible. Then when they don't pay you have to change from the Mr Nice Guy to Mr Dirty. This is what business is all about.

Tony: That is why a lot of people use third parties such as collection agencies or solicitors because it saves them having to deal with that side of things. We have a strategy where we go hard, the debtor rings our client and the client goes soft. The client gets fed up and goes hard on the debtor, the debtor rings us and we go soft. At each stage it should be progressive.

On the soft side, particularly when a debtor is talking to you, then you must try and come to some sort of arrangement. However, if you are going for a short, sharp shock of a *blitzkrieg* approach, then you basically have to take abuse if it comes to you. We also try our best every now and then to tell debtors what they ought to be doing and where they have gone wrong, and we tell our client that (for example) his debtor won't be able to pay for, say, the computer equipment for at least a year. The client in that case wouldn't have given the credit. But that wasn't probably the debtor's intention from the outset. We try and push them, tempt them into trusting us to do a deal and sort it out for them.

And there is always this firm–soft–firm–soft approach in terms of psychology, going on all the time. Personally, I enjoy the telephone, pit-bull-terrier approach. You have to be quite quick on your feet.

Now *we* also get debts too. You may think that funny. Here we are a firm of debt-collection solicitors, and we have debts run up with us. Only two years ago we had a substantial client go down owing us a lot of money. And it hurts. But it was a limited company and we knew the answers better than others.

The debt-collection procedures we adopt for our own money is telephone chasing, trying to understand why it has not been paid and getting into a relationship with the person who is going to pay it. We will in fact send a motor-bike courier to go out and collect it. We put work into a case, spending money on court fees and so on. So we may ask the client to pay something in advance.

Patrick: Would you say that race has got anything to do with the question of debt? In other words is there a race of people who are notorious for bad debts?

Tony: I would say that it is symptomatic throughout all races. A debtor is a debtor. And the sooner you can spot it the better. The problem we have is being English and dealing with a debtor of a different race. Very often we find we don't know whom we are talking to. There are specialist agencies who deal with different

types of debtor in terms of race, because they understand the culture. There are some cultures, for example, who like to barter. They may say, "O.K., Mr Sutton, now that you've got me, let's sort this out. How much do you want?" And then I would say, "I want this much — £100 to start off." And then he would say, "Well, I don't have that amount. Will your client take £50?" I would say,"I doubt it very much."

Then he may say, "Will he take £70?" And they barter. You end up having gone through all these procedures and find that they are bartering as you are moving along. There is certainly an ethnic difference on that. But it is true that there are some ethnic communities who are better at bartering than others. English people by and large, if they cannot pay, will tell you straight that they cannot pay; they stop at that and will accept the action you are trying to take.

Raw nerves

Patrick: Now, Tony, we have covered a lot of ground. The next point I would like to discuss is the question of the stress that people are usually under when they are in debt. Do you experience anxiety in debtors, and how is it portrayed when you are chasing them for money?

Tony: We have had people crying, and flying off the handle at us. We've pursued people, whom we subsequently got to know, who were old and infirm and should never have been chased in the first place by the client. We've had sad stories where the debtor truly had hit hard times and was in a bad way. Well, I'll tell you one.

Because we are a firm of debt recovery solicitors, we had a debtor come to us and ask for our advice on how to deal with many creditors of his. He said: "I want to speak to you, because only you know what is the best course of action for me." I spent an hour with him. We concluded he was bankrupt. He had taken the loan of all loans to pay off his debt. His wife had been made redundant, he had become ill and couldn't work, and they had just about had it. They were paying £5 here and £2 there — they were getting nowhere. Then one year they owed the finance company more than they owed at the beginning despite the fact that they were paying them £20 to £30 a month. They had done their best, and they were not resolving their problem and I said to him, "I wouldn't want to do it, but you are insolvent — you are bankrupt. If I were you,

I would make myself bankrupt and you would be amazed how these creditors will soon disappear." He went and did it and soon his creditors all vanished. I bumped into him a year and a half later in a pub, and suddenly this pint of beer arrived on my table and he thanked me profusely. All the trouble and hassle he was going through at the end of the day was achieving nothing but getting him more ill with worry and anxiety.

Patrick: How does a guy make himself bankrupt?

Tony: Well, he goes to the court, pays a fee, and says "I am who I am and I can't pay my debts. And I would like the court to make an order making me bankrupt." But going back to the stress factor — people can get very emotive. You get people crying, shouting, hurling abuse, putting the phone down — it is all part and parcel of it.

In certain situations, if you persist you can suddenly get that nerve in the debtor that is the one that makes him twitch and sign the cheque. What that is can vary. I remember a debtor once ringing our firm; he had never had a Winding-Up Petition before and asked me what it was all about. I told him what it was. He said he had never seen one of these before, but that he'd better pay it, and he did. He said the reason why he never paid was because he threw all his summonses in the bin — he only paid when he got the bailiff's notices through. And he knew the bailiffs personally because they visited him regularly. What caused a change in his attitude was encountering some procedure that he did not have experience of. Suddenly you strike a nerve, a fear. It could be that his wife accidentally sees his post and notices he is in trouble and gives him stick. It could be any one of a number of things.

Action checklist

Patrick: Tony, I feel that you have covered this topic in a most comprehensive way. Is there anything else you feel you have not covered from your side?

Tony: I think I have covered everything.

Patrick: So if you have to sum up how a creditor can safeguard his payments, what advice can you give the reader of **PAY UP!** Can you please do it in a checklist format?

Tony: O.K.

1. The first thing would be to ask yourself, "Who am I dealing with and who is going to pay my bill? Are they a limited company? If not, who are the individuals involved?"
2. Then ask: "When are they going to pay me?" And if they don't pay you, set up a standard set of procedures that you religiously adopt for all accounts that go overdue.
3. You follow up with a series of letters and phone calls. At each stage, if you don't get through on the phone, putting it in writing is always a good thing — document what you do.
4. Try and get an admission out of the debtor, either in writing or confirmed by you, that he owes you the money and that there is no dispute.
5. Try and get him to tell you the reason why he is not paying you. If possible, visit your debtor at some stage, more importantly to

get to know what it is you are pursuing — he could be living in a caravan, a garden shed, a mansion in St George's Hill, Weybridge. You won't know until you go there — all you do know is that you have dealt with him on the phone. Draw your conclusions from his lifestyle. If, say, he can afford to live in a mansion with some smart cars parked in front, one would hope that he has enough money to pay you, but has chosen not to do so. In other words, he would be worthwhile pursuing as opposed to a guy running a little engineering works in a back street who clearly is doing his best — which in turn would be different from a guy who is running his business from his bedroom and a filing cabinet.
In other words, do your fact-finding before you put your strategy into place.

6. Then decide what your strategies are going to be to collect the debt. That strategy must be appropriate to the type of debtor and the type of debt you are dealing with. The more commercial the debt, the harder you should be. The more personal the debt, in other words if you are dealing with individuals, the more understanding must you be.
7. If a debtor asks for time to pay, don't just shut the door on him. Sort something out. Because nowadays when people say they can't pay the chances are that they are probably right. But you have got to test that it is so.
8. Look out for clues. If he says he is owed money by someone — who is it? Suggest you may be able to help, then you can go and garnishee his debtor.
9. If he owns a house, carry out a Land Regis-

try search. See if he owns the property. If the debtor owns the property you could apply to the court for a Charging Order. If the court grants it and if there is sufficient equity in the property, you could get paid through its sale by permission of the court. This, however, is a complicated procedure and involves issuing further court proceedings.

10. So it is essentially knowing what you are doing. And once you decide on what you are going to do, you just do it. But don't go to your solicitors before doing the groundwork. The more information you are able to give your lawyers, the easier is it for them to adopt procedures that don't waste your money.
11. And the more enthusiastic you are with your lawyer, if they are like us, the better response you will get.

Patrick: And would I be right in saying that you should not put too much faith in the law when it comes to debt recovery?

Tony: The law is a set of procedures you use, hoping that the debtor will pay. There is no guarantee he will pay. A debtor's ability to pay his debt is only as good as the amount he is influenced to do so. And in the final analysis it all depends on him. It may be that a garnishee or a Charging Order just strikes that chord, and he says, "I've had enough, I'll write this cheque out now."

Patrick: And having said all that you have, Tony, in an enlightening way, the message to any debtor must be: "In God we trust, but everyone else must pay by cash." And my advice to any debtor who is relentlessly pursued for payment is, tell your creditor — "I can only afford to pay you £3 a month (or the smallest amount you can afford to give away), but for you I will give £4 (a small additional amount especially for him or her)." That should very diplomatically get your creditor or the debt collector off your back.

Tony: I would like to end up by saying, "Good luck!" because whatever you do there is an element of luck in debt recovery, and it is in the lap of the gods whether you get paid or not. Another point is that in collecting a debt you have to be a bit of a salesman yourself. You have to understand debtor psychology and sell the idea to him of paying the debt. Now he has got to buy that idea and does that by writing a cheque. And unless you can combine salesmanship with the various procedures you adopt in a phone call with him, then you are not going to sell him that idea. And so there is quite a lot of salesmanship in the process. So getting paid is exactly on the same level as selling a product, service or idea. And if you don't get paid, then you are not in business and you are going downhill.

How Customs and Excise get their VAT payments

VAT (Value Added Tax) law requires the trader to pay Customs and Excise the VAT that is owed to them. Generally speaking, that money has got to be paid by the due date, which is normally one month following the end of the VAT tax quarter — most VAT is paid that way. There is, however, a scheme to pay monthly for small businesses called the "annual accounting scheme".

If you do not pay them on time, then you will be running into a debt situation which Customs and Excise will not permit to continue. One of Customs and Excise's main priorities is the collection of VAT, and they have a duty to protect the revenue and maintain its level and flow. If a trader gets into serious debt, Customs and Excise will undertake measures to recover the debt and to prevent its repetition in the future. To that end, they will undertake negotiations with the trader to recover the outstanding money.

If the arrangements agreed to at the end of the day prove unsuccessful and all other means of recovery have been exhausted, they will take the trader to civil court. In extreme cases Customs and Excise would either seek bankruptcy or liquidation of the business. That would achieve two ends:

1. part-recovery of the debt — full recovery not being possible;
2. prevention of recurrence of the debt.

This would fulfil the department's responsibility to protect the revenue.

Here is a real-life example. A trader who defaulted in paying Customs and Excise their VAT got a rude awakening when they arrived on the doorstep of his family business one morning with a truck, distress bailiffs and police. They cleared every single item he had for sale off the shelves, and left him only with the bare essentials, including his wife and children.

The moral of that story is: **Be wise — don't mess about with Customs and Excise!**

A private detective's approach to chasing debts

Many creditors on their own behalf, and the legal establishment, employ private detectives to do the footwork, door-knocking and fact-finding necessary to reclaim money from debtors. This involves public contact and is potentially the most volatile aspect of the business, so one might think it would require the Tarzan type of individual to do it. That is not the case.

To discover what kind of person does this job and to get familiar with some of their tactics — information which can help both creditor and debtor alike — I interviewed Ian Beim, a Member of the Association of British Investigators and a man with considerable experience in the field, so much so that he has been featured on BBC television.

The nature of the work

Patrick: Ian, you are a private detective with considerable expertise and experience in the field of debt recovery. Can you tell me something about your kind of work and how you go about it?

Ian: Certainly. I concentrate mainly on commercial debt recovery, on behalf of large organisations directly or solicitors representing them. And that could involve anything from the tracing of directors of companies and the location and repossession of assets to the serving of legal documents for the recovery of monies. The majority of my work is connected with civil actions for recovering monetary claims on behalf of my clients, who could either be the creditors themselves or their solicitors.

The best approach

Patrick: Over the ten years in which you have been doing this work you must have encountered some dangerous and exciting situations when you presented yourself at the door of the debtor. I guess you may have experienced all sorts of reaction patterns towards you. Can you describe the range of behaviour that you have to deal with?

Ian: It varies every time because you have no idea who you are going to meet or what the circumstances are going to be. All you have is an address and you are aware of what you are trying to achieve. You might have what appears to be a normal address which turns out to be a gypsy camp. So what you might have thought was a normal quiet job could turn out to be just the opposite.

Patrick: As you are dealing with people in the adverse debt situation, what would you say is the main reaction that you get when you arrive on their doorstep? Is it one of friendliness, or antagonism, towards you?

Ian: I have over the years developed a procedure which has worked quite well for me. I started this job in my late teens; I found that when I was younger it wasn't that difficult — because of my age people did not firstly expect to find a young guy doing this sort of job, and they also thought that I did not have any experience to go with it. So they treated me lightly and it was easier to achieve my objectives.

But as I have got older, people seem to be prepared to be more aggressive and make it harder for me. They treat me like an equal. I have counteracted that by being so polite — in fact over-polite — that it virtually makes it impossible for them to be awkward towards me.

Patrick: So what you are saying is that in any situation where you are confronting a debtor, "Politeness" is a cardinal rule.

Ian: Yes. I would also recommend going on your own, because people are naturally intimidated if there are more people than yourself standing on their doorstep. I would be ridiculously polite to them. I would apologise for troubling them. I would call them "Sir" or "Madam" so that I do not give them a chance to become aggressive to me. So I am able to approach 99 per cent of the people I deal with in a civilised manner; but having said that, you will come across that 1 per cent who will hit anyone who comes to their door anyway.

Patrick: This would mean that you play a very submissive role with debtors, to achieve your objectives.

Ian: Correct. If you let them think they have got the upper hand because you are apologetic for troubling them, you get them on your side.

They then start to co-operate and you can therefore acquire what you set out to achieve. You gain their confidence by acting like this, as opposed to putting on an image of bravado and trying to assert yourself in a macho way. That approach often turns out to be counterproductive — they begin to get defensive under those conditions.

Patrick: From what you have told me it appears that your method of tackling the situation is quite the reverse of what many people think debt collection is all about. That is, they imagine you have to be a strapping "bouncer" type of guy, who walks up, flexes his muscles and more-or-less brow-beats the debtor into paying up. The impression I get is that by adopting your approach, you make the debtor feel big while you play the humble, non-threatening investigator, and you eventually get what you want out of him by playing the nice guy.

Ian: The secret of success in this business is just that. In the back of my mind I know what I am trying to achieve. When I gain their confidence they are no longer being defensive — then I go on the offensive.

However, I must admit that there are some people doing this work who do use heavy-handed tactics. But I couldn't do that because (as you can see) I am not heavily built. About 50 per cent of the people I see are bigger than me. But it doesn't really pay to be the tough guy. You can beat a guy's head in with a cricket bat, but that is not necessarily going to make him co-operate. If, on the other hand, you have won his confidence — or even if you unfortunately haven't — by being nice to him, you might get him to give you some spiel which could be telling you something you wanted to know. He would do this because in this way he would feel he was asserting himself over you. You are always going to be more successful using your wits as opposed to resorting to violence.

Patrick: You have told me that in the main you do not use the aggressive approach. Is this something that you have learned over the years through experience? For example, is it that you started off by being aggressive, then found it did not work so mellowed down? Or is that just your nature? Or is it that you have witnessed others who were aggressive and failed, and you learned from their mistakes?

Ian: I wouldn't say being passive is my nature. Running a small, successful business I have got to be assertive and determined to succeed. I must admit I do not enjoy taking the submissive role and doing it that way when dealing with debtors, but I have found that is the way it works for me. I cannot recall ever having been over-forceful with people, because I do not have the size to do it. When I was younger, people may have become suspicious because of my size and age that I was into 'martial' arts. Then again, because I was a young lad they would have thought they were not going to hit someone who was 5′ 7″ who was not their equal. But now, ten years later, if I get it wrong they will have a crack at me.

Patrick: So, in any event, there is always that danger, that if you go in with that intimidating approach you could meet with your Waterloo because the guy who owes you the money could be just as vicious as you are, or possibly even be ten times more dangerous than you are.

Ian: Yes, indeed. Some of the people I go and see can be just like that. For example, I had a case in Wales. The guy had a pit-bull terrier that he tied to a stake on a long chain outside his front door. The chain was about a foot shorter than the distance to his front gate. If you took one step in, the dog would have had you for breakfast.

Then I had a case where I was trying to repossess a truck. I was given the key because it was locked up in a yard. They had dogs roaming about and I had to get in and take it, and it was a race for me to get to the truck before the dogs got to me. As you can imagine I got to the truck first because you can run very fast when you have a dog chasing you!

Strategies for success

Patrick: So you strongly recommend the "soft approach", which I too would endorse as being the better way to handle such situations. Having said that, are there times when you have to be a bit aggressive to show the debtor who you are, to achieve your objectives? In what circumstances would you do that?

Ian: Obviously, you can't let them walk all over you. I think it depends on what you are trying to achieve. If you are trying to interview someone to try and glean information, then it is always better to put them in the driving seat. A classic example is where you tell someone the wrong thing — they will correct you. Say, for example, you wanted to ascertain what someone was doing for a living and you were speaking to his neighbour. You would say something such as: "Is he still a builder?" and they would say: "No, he is not a builder. He is a milkman."

Patrick: In the selling profession we call that the erroneous conclusion technique.

Ian: There are some circumstances where you have to play it that way. Then there are other situations where you have to take a statement from someone, so you have to be courteous with them because you want them to cooperate with you. But at the same time you have to ascertain the details your client wants.

I suppose the time when you have to be most forceful is when you are serving them with legal documents such as summonses, writs and so on, when they won't accept them. Good service does not mean that they accept the documents in their hands without paying attention to them. What it does mean is that the documents are brought to their attention in their presence and they understand what they have received. If they turn around and say that they are not going to accept the papers, then I wouldn't take them back — I would drop them at their feet, throw them through the letterbox, or whatever. I would take that kind of positive action in that situation because nine times out of ten they are refusing to accept the service only because they want to avoid the matter.

Bailiffs

Patrick: How does your work differ from that of a bailiff?

Ian: Well, there are various kinds of work that bailiffs do. There is the County Court bailiff who is instructed to levy against goods at a certain address. There are different kinds of bailiffing inasmuch as there are different kinds of warrants.

I am not an expert on bailiffs' work. You may have seen on TV the commercial bailiffs who are employed by councils to collect council tax and rent arrears.

The County Court bailiffs are employed on a full-time basis and work for the public. For example, if you sue someone and get judgement, and if the other party does not respond, then you can instruct the court bailiff to go to their house by paying the court an additional fee. Then the bailiff will go and withdraw sufficient goods, to the value of the money owed.

Working for companies

Patrick: When your clients bypass the legal establishment and come to you direct, what do you do for them?

Ian: Almost every company in business has its own credit control department. This is irrespective of the fact that it could be Joe Bloggs trading on his own and every Thursday afternoon he is trying to collect his outstanding invoices. Then again it could be a multi-million-pound company that has an entire section as the credit control division.

The bigger companies tend to have a credit manager who might be conversant with some of the legal procedures. He may very well issue the County Court summons to their debtors himself. If it is contested, he may well pass the matter over to the company's solicitors. I may be involved if the company is attempting to get monies and the correspondence is returned. They may instruct me to find out where the people have moved to, or if they are still there. Or they may be reluctant to pass it on to their solicitors without establishing some form of status, and therefore do not want to incur further costs in trying to do so. In other words, I could be employed directly by the company at that stage to do the legwork and fact-finding; after I report back to them, then they would instruct their solicitors.

The solicitor would then have a more accurate idea of how to tackle the matter. For example, he/she might want to issue a Charging Order on the property, whereas the client may want only to secure the payment of the money owed. So the solicitor may do a Land Registry search and discover that the property is not registered. So they employ me to find out the identity of the owners. The way I would do that is to make discreet inquiries with the debtor's neighbours and confirm who lived at that address. Then I would go there and ask for somebody completely different; and understandably, they would deny all knowledge of such a person. Then I would engage them in conversation: "Well, I am sure it was this number — you've been here long? — Are you the owners, or is there a landlord?" They may reply, "We are Mr and Mrs Jones, the owners. We bought it from a Mr Smith five years ago — that other name you had was wrong."

You now know who lives at the address because you confirmed it with their neighbours, and for how long they've owned the property. So you extract information and build up a picture of the people you are concerned with.

If you look at each piece of information as parts of a jigsaw, there is obviously an end-result you want to achieve. Between the point of making the sale and getting paid, there could be a hiccup. So I will be employed in between to sort out any snags. For example, if they return the invoice unpaid, I will try to establish what went wrong and try to sort it out in the best possible way to facilitate payment.

Patrick: Now you have explained your job function very clearly to me. You are saying that after the sale has been made, the getting-paid part of it can become a completely separate complex matter, and of a protracted nature. In other words, after you have sold something things can start to run in a different direction when it comes to collecting the payment, which can cost the seller further time, money and anxiety to recover.

Ian: The problem with a lot of companies, both big and small, is that they put a lot of emphasis on sales and do not pay too much attention to the credit-control side of the business. This easy-going attitude to payment collection has probably changed a lot in these recessionary times because companies now realise how important cash flow is to their survival. In pre-recession times, if they got paid 85 per cent of their sales, they could afford to wait longer for the 15 per cent balance or even possibly to lose it in extreme cases. But that type of thinking is now changing rapidly, with companies taking a pro-active role to recover any monies due to them by all the means they have at their disposal.

In pre-recession times, the banks and the building societies were giving away money because they could afford to do so as business was so good — they could afford to take the risk then. However, the general type of debtor has changed dramatically in recent times. Nowadays, the average debtor is genuine and hasn't got the money to pay back. When he/she borrowed the money to buy something, he/she had every intention of paying it back — but since then he/she has been made redundant (or whatever) and cannot honour his/her commitments.

In pre-recession times companies could afford to be rather blasé with users of their credit facilities. They did not apply the pre-credit check criteria stringently. As a consequence, the type of client who made use of the credit facility regularly turned out to be the person who intentionally did not want to pay back the borrowed money — he/she could go to the ABC Bank and then to the XYZ Bank and get horrendous amounts of money unsecured. So borrowers got the money, got the goods and then didn't pay for it. These days it is more difficult to get money because the lending institutions have learnt their lesson. Banks and finance houses are now very cautious about to whom they lend. So now you are faced with a more genuine kind of debtor. That would be the case in the short term, as I see it. But in the long term, when the financial situation in the country improves, people will start to use credit again, but I do not think it will get back to the situation of the mid to late 1980s. And when things do get better, the intentional, seasoned debtors (as I call them) will come out of the woodwork again.

The seasoned debtor

Patrick: If you were to give a profile of this type of debtor — the hard nut who doesn't "give a cuss" about the consequences of, say, getting goods and not paying for them — how would you describe him? Can you give me some examples on how you've dealt with this type?

Ian: I am not so sure that I can give a definite profile. Such a person could be living on the eighteenth floor of a block of flats in the Isle of Dogs. They may have borrowed money and cannot pay it back. So the attitude I would encounter when I go there is, "We don't have anything and we can't pay for it and that's it. So you can do what you like." Another theory of mine relates to outstanding loans and finance agreements. They may have initially taken out a credit agreement intending to pay it back. But once the novelty of the goods purchased wears off, people get bored and they don't want to continue paying for something they no longer want or consider important.

From seeing thousands and thousands of such cases, I would say that it is not the case that they can't pay, but it is more the case where they don't want to pay. It is the same philosophy — although people won't admit to it — if for example you have to give details in court of your financial situation when you are fined for a motoring offence: you make yourself as poor as possible so that you get the minimum fine. A lot of people do that. These are games that people play, but who's going to admit it? At the other end of the scale you have the "Yuppie debtor". He is the status man with much bigger borrowings. He would have a BMW or a couple of big cars on HP. He has an enormous house with everything you could ask for. He just wants to be seen with all those trappings. Whereas another guy may not be after the status symbols, but just wants the money to have a good time, and after he gets it he spends it and is in Cloud Cuckoo Land, not having the means or knowledge on how to pay it back. Bear in mind, amongst any of these people can be the 1 per cent who are the aggressive type.

Aggressive responses

Patrick: Have you ever been punched? Under what circumstances did that happen?

Ian: The first time I was ever punched was when I was collecting £100 for a lease company for a cash register in a retail shop. An argument started between me and the debtor over how long he was taking to count the money out in £1 coins. He was making it as difficult as possible for me to get the money and eventually we both got a bit frustrated. So I asked him politely to hurry up as I had other appointments to go to, at which point he said, "In that case, take this and go!" and he landed me a big punch on my face. I was stunned.

Patrick: And what did you do?

Ian: I hit him back. It ended by his wife intervening

and breaking it up. Then I picked up the money and took off.

This kind of circumstances you can never predict. I once served legal documents on a chef working in a big hotel near Heathrow Airport. He became violent towards me and came at me wielding this big knife. He had to be restrained by the other members of staff.

Patrick: Did you run away?

Ian: I did not. No matter how worried you are, you must not panic and run away from them, because you might have to go back. Some of these people I deal with may crop up four or five times in the course of my work. We are talking here about intentional debtors. I might be working on behalf of one client, and then all of a sudden I am doing work on the same debtor for another client . . . and another client . . . and so on.

So, it all goes back to being polite. If I am aggressive with someone, then two weeks later I have to see him again for another client and I have fallen out with him, it is going to be even worse for me. It pays to be diplomatic with debtors. Going back to the point you mentioned about running away — if I did that, it would give them the upper hand: they would feel confident, and they would try to run all over me.

I had to go to a farm in Hull earlier this year, where the person I had to see was doing some welding at the back of the farmhouse. He had a few friends with him — they were the traveller type. No sooner had I introduced myself to him, extremely politely, then he came at me with the blowtorch, aiming it at my face. That was an instant reaction on his part. He said in strong language to me: "If you don't f...... remove yourself from here, I will set light to you." I pointed out that he was already trying to do that! The funniest part of it was that when I was making my way back, I saw the old man in the front who had told me where this guy was when I entered. When he saw me returning he asked me whether I had seen the person I had come to see. I said yes, and that he had tried to set light to me. And the old man replied: "Oh yes, he would do!"

Patrick: So, Ian, you have given me three cases of the aggressive reaction patterns. Are there any more?

Ian: Yes, I have more. I had a case where I was trying to repossess a tractor unit. It was in Liverpool. Unknown to me the finance company had told the debtor that they knew friends of the notorious Krays and that if he did not pay up they were going to send someone around to sort him out — I was that person. I went there in the daytime, but he was out and his wife asked me to come back later. When I returned later he was waiting with a baseball bat to use my head as a baseball!

Patrick: So what did you do then?

Ian: Well, I actually used my diplomacy and my apologetic approach, and came out with a cheque for £1000 and no bruises.

Then, around 1985, I had a big case — to collect money from a reputed international pop group of Rastafarians who owed money to a recording studio. It was the equivalent of an English writ that was issued in one of the States in America. I had to serve each member of the band with one of these. Because they all looked alike it was rather difficult to distinguish who was who, and furthermore they were not co-operating with me. They were on their way to the Glastonbury Pop Festival and I was staying at the same hotel as they were. There were about seven or eight of them, but they did not reveal their identities to me. However, I managed to get three of them.

Then, I sweet-talked the hotel receptionist into giving me a list of their bedrooms and the names of the occupants. I went around at about six o'clock in the morning disguised as Room Service, and knocked on their doors. I served them all with the writs, and served them to the right individuals because I had all the information with me. All of them accepted it except one. He was a big guy who put his fist against my face and said he was going to punch me, which fortunately he didn't. It was a great success. I was very happy, but they weren't.

Patrick: When they become physical, does it frighten you or do you laugh it off lightly?

Ian: It can become frightening. I would be lying if I said that it didn't. However, when serving legal documents you must adopt a stubborn approach. In this instance this big guy put his fist up to me and said that he would hit me if I tried to serve it on him. But I insisted that I was not going to take it back — I have never taken one back in my life. So I dropped it and walked off. Someone would have to put a gun to my head for me to change my approach, but — touch wood — that has not happened so far!

But I have had situations where people have threatened me by phoning me or my wife and saying that if I ever went back to see them they would blow off my kneecaps and that sort of thing.

If they are not there when I go to see them, I leave my card with my telephone number and address. It annoys me when someone rings my wife, for example, instead of talking to me, and says something like: "Your husband has annoyed someone and he is going to get his kneecaps blown off", because that frightens her.

Questions of identity

Patrick: Now let's move on from these aggressive reactions that you've encountered, to some of the sly or cunning things that debtors do to prevent you from achieving your objective.

Ian: I suppose the most common one is to use an alias. You have to be very careful when you are asking for someone by name, to make sure you do it precisely, almost pedantically, so

that they cannot find a way to wriggle out. Say, for example, I am looking for Joseph George Bloggs; when I call at his home, I introduce myself and ask for Mr Bloggs and he doesn't want to see me, so he says: "Ah the person you want is Joe Bloggs. I am Harry Bloggs."
At the same time, you don't want to be too official and come out straight and say, "Can I speak to Mr Joseph George Bloggs?" That approach would obviously scare him and put him on guard so that he wouldn't co-operate. After all, if a stranger walked to your door with a piece of paper in their hand and asked to speak to you, you would automatically be defensive because you would think, "Here comes trouble!" So if I have got any legal documents to serve, I always keep them in my pocket and I always dress according to the surroundings. I only dress formally if I am visiting a big corporation. In other words I always try not to appear official, because the moment they think you are official, that's it — they don't want to speak to you. If I said: "Can I speak to Mr Joe Bloggs?" he would say, "Who wants him? — What's it about?" People become so suspicious. So the way I would tackle it is to say: "Can I speak to Joseph Bloggs please?" By playing it down like that, I would get the required reaction for setting up a meaningful dialogue.
There was a guy to whom I had to serve some documents only last week. There are certain kinds of documents you can leave in the letterbox in an envelope addressed to the debtors as long as you know that it will come to their attention. The wife answered the door and I asked to speak to her husband. She said, "I'll just get him for you." The guy came to the door and I started talking to him about it. He

said, "I am not accepting anything here — it has got to be delivered to my business address." So I asked him what the business address was. He said, "I am not going to tell you." "In that case," I told him, "how could I go there without the details?" He was obviously trying to evade the issue. He said it would have to be served by post. I said that it had already been served by post to this address and it had been returned marked "Gone away". Now I had taken the precaution of bringing the documents to him in the envelope already sealed. So I started taking them out in front of him. He said, "Don't do that! It is mine, it is private and it is addressed to me." So I told him, "As you are not telling me where to serve this, I am dropping it at your feet now." He replied, "You can't do that as you haven't confirmed the name of the guy it is addressed to." So I said: "Yes I have, because you just told me not to open the envelope as it was addressed to you."

Patrick: That was an interesting little example. You were telling me earlier on about an incident which occurred overseas. What exactly happened?

Ian: I have worked both in Spain and in France. Investigators have to be licensed to work there. I had an assignment in Paris which was not properly organised. It was a matrimonial case — not my favourite subject. It started in London, but moved to Paris. The man owed maintenance money over here to his ex-wife, but did a vanishing trick and was with another woman. I was required to see the solicitor in Paris who was acting on behalf of my client. When I got there he hadn't the documents, so I had to fly back to London to fetch them and return to Paris that same afternoon.

The couple concerned were thought to be putting up in a top hotel. When I checked their whereabouts at Reception, they confirmed that the people I was looking for were there, but there was a slight error in the way the man's name was spelled, compared with the spelling I had — one letter was different, giving the wrong pronunciation. It turned out that the person I had been pursuing for three days was entirely the wrong one. It was a case of mistaken identity. So I could not serve the documents.

There was another case which I handled in Spain. It was to do with breach of contract. There were two top-level directors of a company who both left at the same time and were believed to be setting up in competition with their employers. One of the directors went to Barcelona and the other went to Amsterdam. I was sent to do the investigation in Barcelona to try and establish what exactly was happening, on behalf of my client, the company concerned. As is often the case for such high-ranking employees, it had been stipulated in their contracts of employment that if they left the company they were not to set up in direct competition with that company within a certain time of leaving or within a specified distance; this was to safeguard the company's business interests.

My problem was that I could not speak Spanish, although I had someone with me who could. However, the most interesting aspect of this case was how I turned my inability to speak this language to my advantage. I knew where the guy was living. It is relatively easy to follow someone, to sit down and observe them, on the Continent because there are cafés and bars everywhere. I followed this ex-director to where he was working. It turned out to be an area of office blocks with a number of companies in it.

On Day 1, my first step was to find out which building he was going into and what car he was driving. On Day 2, the following morning, I positioned myself in a café opposite his place of work and saw him arrive. But I went into the building dressed in a suit and tie, in front of him. Despite the fact that there was security in the building, I looked straight ahead and gave the impression I knew where I was going, even though I had never been in there before. Nobody challenged me. Now I was in the building before him so he did not suspect that

I was following him. Likewise, I got into the lift in front of him and pressed the button for the top floor.

He pressed the third floor button — there was no way he knew he was being observed at close quarters. So now I knew which building he worked in, and what floor he worked on. My next task was to find out which company he worked for on the third floor.

Because I did not speak Spanish I acted as stupid and as ignorant as possible so that people I talked to started getting angry. When they are angry they are not concentrating, and they get frustrated and start to tell you things you want to know. I kept repeating that I was trying to contact a friend of mine — I made up a fictitious name. They did not believe it. So I produced a piece of paper with the fictitious name and the address of their building on it, which I said somebody had given me over the phone, and which I showed to the taxi driver who dropped me there. Now everyone in Reception was trying to help me out and I started to learn things I wanted to know. They started telling me there is this company on this floor, and that company on that floor. And the only English man in the building was working on the third floor, for the XYZ Company. I had cracked it once I knew which company he worked for, because from that information it would be possible to establish his activities and the company's business.

So the essence of that case was that I used my inability to speak Spanish to two distinct advantages. People first felt sympathetic towards me and tried to help me out. Then, when I wanted more information, I purposely acted outrageously stupid so that they got exasperated to the point where they gave me the information I wanted, just to get rid of me. That worked out very well for me.

In the UK you could do a company search, at Companies House, Crown Way, Maindy, Cardiff CF4 3UZ. You can go there and find out all the information from the file, such as what the main activities of the company are and what its turnover is. There will be details of the board of directors and shareholders. A similar information file would also exist in Spain, according to their system. Once you establish the company's identity, finding out the rest is paperwork and common sense.

In a slightly different context . . . when I am working here in the UK, suppose that I go into a business to establish whether they are a limited company: the name at the top of their letterhead is their trading name. The company registration number in which I am interested is normally at the bottom. So sometimes when I go in I may end up talking a whole lot of rubbish with a member of staff just to keep them going till I memorise the company registration number. It has become such a strong habit with me that I cannot go into anyone's home or office without trying in one way or another to get hold of their company registration number!

Patrick: So, in other words, the nature of your work is such that your eyes are searching and your ears are listening for information and you think on your feet: then you take a pro-active approach towards achieving your objective.

Ian: All the time. Whenever I go into an office I am automatically searching for a certificate of incorporation, or a licence, or a membership certificate — it is the force of habit, I just can't help it!

Debtors in genuine misfortune

Patrick: Now we have spoken about some of the different types of people and situations that you have experienced. You have been dealing with the aggressive type, the cunning type; what about the timid kind of person who trembles when they know you have landed on their doorstep? It may be the genuine debtor who has got into an adverse financial situation through no fault of their own: they know they owe the money and consequently feel very threatened by your presence. How would you deal with this kind?

Ian: Well, that situation is quite straightforward. They are not so much of a problem. Normally, the majority of people who have genuinely hit hard times will be co-operative. It is the ones who are genuine and stick their heads in the sand who are difficult. It is not the fact that they have a money crisis which could probably be solved. The real problem is that they will not sit down with someone and solve it.

I have a case on now where I have gone to a guy's address about 15 times and every time he is allegedly out. Every time I leave a message for him to contact me, he just ignores it. As far as I am concerned I am going to keep going there till I get through to him, because it has become matter of principle with me now. It is a local job, so I won't really be going out of my way. That will happen till one of us gets bored and gives up.

Then again, on the other side of the coin, you get genuine people for whom it is not so much that they are trying to put their heads in the sand, but that they won't admit to their bad financial circumstances. They've been prosperous in the past, but they won't confess that they've hit hard times. Their pride may be too great.

I have dealt with cases connected with lords, titled people, professional people of all descriptions, chairmen of multi-million-pound companies, armed forces personnel from all ranks (I get those quite regularly — I have been to Sandhurst often!) and so on. I once dealt with a peer who did not even divulge his own identity, let alone admit that he was in financial difficulty. In my opinion, he would not accept the fact that someone such as myself was required to call upon him to recover money that he owed. Then I've dealt with doctors, pharmacists, dentists . . .

Patrick: Dentists could be tough nuts. They will grab your teeth before you extract the money — a little bit of drilling and a little bit of filling for you will save them a painful extraction from their wallet!

Ian: Professional people are not so difficult to tackle because you can contact or locate them through their professional bodies. From time to time I have had to do work on solicitors who have fallen into financial difficulty. You can get through to them quite easily through the Law Society. Not all solicitors deal with litigation and know a lot about it. Professional people in general are quite easy to get hold of because usually they are still trading. And if they are not, they will still be members of their professional body and you can track them down from there. Most professional bodies other than left-wing unions will confirm their membership details over the telephone. The name, address and telephone number of a member can be obtained without difficulty.

A lot of these people fall into financial difficulty because of bad management of their financial affairs, for one reason or another.

Lie detection

Patrick: O.K. Let's proceed to some of the knock-on effects that a debt situation could produce. If, for example, a household hits a financial trouble spot, that in turn could lead to other unpleasant situations. There could be divorces. There is a saying: "When poverty creeps through the door, love flies through the window!" Then children could be separated from their parents. A lot of anxiety and depression can be present. There could be a great deal of upheaval in the debtor's personal and business life.

How would you view those factors, and would it affect you and your work? You may be at the receiving end of as many tales of genuine heartache as of sob-stories.

Ian: Of course I am. I have probably seen thousands and thousands of cases over the last ten years. Nine times out of ten I can figure out whether someone is telling you the truth or not, purely because while it might be the first time they are using that excuse, it may be the third time that I have heard it that day.

Only two weeks ago, in the space of half an hour I had three telephone calls from people I was trying to contact. One was going on holiday and two were going into hospital, all on the same day. That will give you an idea of how many times people whom I contact are going into hospital or on holiday that very afternoon. I have heard that so many times. The country would have collapsed if there were that many people going into hospital or on holiday at that frequency.

So I play it by ear. You become reluctant to believe everything you see and hear. And you become experienced at spotting the genuine cases, as distinct from the ones who are trying to pull a fast one on you. Occasionally I could be wrong, but I am right most of the time — that is what experience is all about.

If I can prove that they are misleading me in the course of my work, then I can report back to my client, saying something such as: "This was what was told to me. However, I have established that so-and-so is not unemployed as he claims and that he is actually working for the ABC Company." It is not my job even to risk giving my client information that could be wrong. I am employed by my client to find out what the situation actually is — what is said, rather than my surmising about it — and then report back the facts as accurately as possible.

Having said that, if as a result of my inquiries during the investigation I suspect something then it is a lot safer to report what I have established as opposed to what I assume to be going on.

Patrick: Do you find that there is a big gap between what you think might be the situation and what it actually is?

Ian: Well, obviously, there can be. For example, somebody might ring you on behalf of the debtor, and you might think that it is his wife, but it might be his mother. So you write back to your client and say that he lives at that address with his wife, but he doesn't. He is in fact living there with his parents. So unless you go and establish that, you would be passing wrong information to your client.

Patrick: So would you say that you approach all investigations with a certain amount of suspicion?

Ian: It does not automatically follow that I do. I am just in a state of heightened awareness, that someone might be trying to mislead me because of the nature of the business I am in. So I keep an open eye and am on the ball when I am working.

Most investigators will probably tell you nine times out of ten, when they come out from an interview, "Heck, why didn't I ask him that question? That always crops up — it didn't occur to me at the time and it would have clarified something that I was not so sure about." If you were discussing something under a false pretext then you might not be able to go back, but if it is to establish a fact you could very well do so.

The good detective

Patrick: If you were to describe a good private detective, what would you say would be the hallmark of such a person?

Ian: I suppose determination and resilience, with an ability to read between the lines of every bit of information you are looking for. For example if, say, you are looking for someone named Joe Bloggs in a telephone directory, you look under "Bloggs" and there is no one with the initial J. So you then look under the other Bloggses — has he got the telephone registered under his wife's initials, which many of this type of crafty character do, in a different initial from their own? You have to keep an open mind all the time. It is like doing a jigsaw puzzle; you have to look at it from different aspects to fit the pieces together.

Patrick: So are you saying to me that in your way of doing things there is always the "cowboys and crooks" approach to life? In other words, nothing is straightforward — wherever there are cowboys and crooks you can expect something dodgy and you must always go prepared for it. So if someone gets into debt, you will always approach the situation with suspicion.

Ian: You don't approach every case with suspicion. But you must be prepared for any eventuality. You have to pre-empt situations and be one step ahead all the time because in a lot of these cases you are only given one crack at it. The best advantage that we have over our opposite number is the element of surprise — someone is not expecting you, he is sitting at home watching the telly with his wife and kids at 8.30 p.m., and you knock on the door. Let me not startle you; I often start work at 6.30 a.m. and finish at midnight. I would not knock on someone's door at midnight unless I have to, but I would usually do so up to about 9.30 p.m.

So the best approach would be to catch people off their guard, introducing an element of surprise by asking: "Can I speak to Joe Bloggs?" The automatic reply would be: "Yes, that's me." Yet if I was standing at his front door with a sheet of paper in my hand, appearing official, he would become defensive, possibly "switch off" and try to get rid of me.

I usually see a vast number of people for the first time when they are relaxed, on a one-to-one basis; provided I am polite with them, I often get good results. But as I told you earlier, there is always that 1 per cent who, no sooner than they see you, will come at you like a viper.

Patrick: Just to recap on the points that go make a good private detective. You said they are:

1. Determination.
2. The ability to read between the lines.
3. The use of the element of surprise.
4. Politeness.
5. The capacity to be one step ahead of the situation and make viable decisions on the spur of the moment.

Are there any other qualities that spring to your mind?

Ian: Well, apart from the attributes of being able to run a business — a good number of them have gone down in the recession — and being a workhorse with a sense of independence and initiative and able to work on your own, there are not many other qualities that I can think of. You cannot plan for what people are going to say to you, so you have to live on your wits.

Patrick: I notice that you are a Member of the Association of British Investigators. Are there any formal qualifications that are required to become a private detective?

Ian: There are no formal qualifications necessary. However, you do have to sit an entrance examination. You would be required to have practised, or at least to have been employed, in an investigative position for a minimum of two years and you would be asked to supply references. Having said this, membership is not subject to legislation and not therefore compulsory. Anyone can set up to provide status enquiries for clients for credit referrals, but you must be licensed by the Office of Fair Trading and have a Consumer Credit Licence to do this work. We are just like a financial adviser — a consumer credit broker — who also needs a Consumer Credit Licence to operate. But we are at the other end of the business.

Patrick: Do you also counsel on debt problems?

Ian: No, but clearly I have covered myself with all the right information as a category of my licence, just in case it backfired and somebody said that I was giving them wrong advice. But the two main categories are credit rating (credit reference) and debt collection. The Association of British Investigators, along with the Institute of Professional Investigators, are the two prominent voluntary bodies who represent our interests.

Patrick: This profession of yours is made up of a lot of ex-policemen — is that right?

Ian: Yes. A good number are retired policemen because it is something in which they have some relevant experience. And they could be from any rank.

Telephone bugs

Patrick: Now you have been on the BBC *Terry Wogan Show* and *Reportage*. What made the Wogan show get interested in your work?

Ian: I believe their objective was to ascertain if there was any similarity between police work and that of investigators.

Patrick: In your work, do you get involved in bugging phones?

Ian: No, but I have worked quite a lot with counter electronic surveillance, which is de-bugging.

Patrick: Can you explain?

Ian: Bugging can be anything from a telephone bug to a rifle mike (microphone). These days it is all hi-tech stuff. You can have a bug which has its own power source which is battery-operated and lasts for a few hours. For example, you might want to record a board meeting and you know when it is going to take place. You can then set the bugging device up, conceal it and, depending on the power, it will start to transmit up to a certain distance the conversations which you can pick up from, say, a car radio outside the building.

You can aim the rifle mike at a location in the building and pick up conversations. Obviously it works best in places where there isn't too much background disturbance such as the movement of cars, buses and lorries. But the bugs themselves can come in many forms. I have seen them in plugs, lamps and so on. These bugs get their power through electricity. So, if there is a meeting, the lamp will be switched on. That will give the bugging device its power source and then you can pick up the information.

To counter this there is de-bugging equipment available. For example, you can fit a device which will cut off a telephone conversation if it is being recorded. You can get various machines which will pick up signals from a transmitting bug. Normally the equipment is best described as looking like a portable radio which searches various waveband frequencies and gives a high-pitched howling noise. In a de-bugging situation, you would put it in a room, switch it on and it would search making this whining noise. It has a dial that will tune into different frequencies and if it picks up an active device, it will start screeching. If you point its antenna in the direction of the bug, the noise will increase as you get nearer to it. So you can track it down.

As I told you earlier, I have not been connected with the bugging side, but I have worked on a number of occasions on the de-bugging side, conducting electronic sweeps for clients situated in buildings in the City of London. I could be employed before an important meeting or to do a routine sweep of their premises every six months.

Patrick: So this type of electronic warfare is going on in British business regularly?

Ian: Yes. That is right. There is a big market out there for that sort of work.

Advice to debtors

Patrick: We have discussed a lot of different things, Ian. It has been very informative. Let's take the debtor's view for a moment. Firstly, what can debtors do, to avoid further trouble, when they are being pursued ruthlessly for payment by their creditors? And secondly, what would your advice be to them if they have a private detective or a debt collector on their doorstep?

Ian: My plain and simple advice would be to try as much as possible to avoid getting into that awkward situation. This means that you have to manage your financial affairs more efficiently. But as we have discussed earlier, there are two categories: there are the genuine people who can't help being in that position because of some misfortune that befell them, and then there are the opportunists who get into the debt situation for their own benefit. Provided you are genuine, the best advice I can give is "Don't stick your head in the sand." As long as you communicate all the time with your creditors and tell them the truth about your financial circumstances, you will find that they have neither the need nor the inclination to issue proceedings against you. In such circumstances, nine times out of ten you will find them sympathetic towards you. Co-operate at all times with your creditors. In doing so, you will save them time and money and they will be more favourable towards you. It is when a debtor claims he has no source of income and the creditor finds out that he is doing paid work that the problems start — they will then pursue you more vigorously.

The difficulty lies with people who, though they are genuine, just won't face up to reality, and hope the debt problem will go away. That won't happen. The more you avoid it, the worse it will get! The more you put it off, the more you owe — the interest builds up. If the creditor issues proceedings through a solicitor, then costs will be involved. So my advice would also be to deal with the matter as quickly as you can. In answer to your second question: if they have a private investigator at their door, they might well not know they are being investigated unless they are being served with legal documents!

Personal disguise

Patrick: That leads me on to the next interesting point. You said that some of the tactics that you use to conceal your identity can appear very simple and inconspicuous, but they are very effective. Can you name a few?

Ian: These methods are used more when I am carrying out an observation, rather than when I am actually calling on someone. For example, I would walk my dog up and down the road in front of the house so that no one would become suspicious of me.

I had a case in Deptford where I knew the debtor was going to be violent towards me.

So I took my baby son who was only a few months old with me, and knocked on the door. When he opened the door and saw me with the baby he just mellowed down; whereas if I had gone on my own he would have been as violent as he could. People tend to be violent towards you if they feel that you are an equal adversary

Problems of gender

Patrick: In your day-to-day work, do you deal mainly with men or with women?

Ian: I would say men. That is not because men are worse at managing their financial affairs. It is more to do with the fact that in the society we live in, with married couples and families, the man is still regarded as the head of the house. He is still seen as the breadwinner; therefore, if there is a financial agreement it is usually taken out in his name.

For the majority of married households in this country, the entry in the telephone directory is in the man's name except when it is specifically requested to be in the wife's name.

Patrick: In the course of your work, have you dealt with women debtors? Do they react differently from men, for instance by becoming emotional, crying, screaming and shouting?

Ian: I suppose it is mixed with women. Some women are not so much aggressive, but they become irate. I don't know whether it is because they resent a man coming round and whether it would be different if I were a woman, or whether my skills are not that good in communicating with them — whatever it may be, I still approach the task in hand in the same way as I would for men, as I described earlier.

Patrick: Has it ever happened that if they couldn't pay you in cash, they offered to pay in kind?

Ian: It hasn't. I'm still waiting!

Patrick: I have heard that it happened to a certain landlord who owned a nice flat, but had an attractive foreign student tenant living in it. She was here to learn English. The rent was overdue by a few weeks, so he went around to collect it. When he asked for it she said she was hard up and that if he searched her trousers he would not find any money in them, but he would discover something better. He replied that he didn't want to do that. Then she offered to pay him partly in cash and partly in fun; and if he was not ageeable to that she was going to leave the country and he would get nothing. She said she could claim diplomatic immunity as her father was working for the Embassy. He had put up with a lot of these sob-stories, so he decided to sell the flat. He advertised it. The first buyer who came round didn't think too much of the flat, but fell head-over-heels over the tenant. He said he would buy it, if he could befriend the tenant. So the landlord sold the flat with the tenant. That was a happy ending to a debt situation!

Some funny business

Patrick: Ian, I feel you have covered your subject comprehensively. Is there anything you feel you have missed out? Are there any other humorous stories you have to relate?

Ian: We have covered all the approaches and ins and outs of my work. I have some other stories to tell. More hairy ones, I suppose — gypsy evictions.

There was a time when I was doing gypsy evictions. I went to an estate where there were gypsies. I became very skilled at evicting the gypsies, but not too good at handling their dogs — I have been bitten a few times. There was an enormous gypsy camp in Edmonton which I had to evict, about a hundred caravans. I cleared the site of all the people, to find that I had a terrier hanging on to the back of my calf. That was funny, but painful too.

I handled that eviction by myself; but if I felt that the situation was going to be volatile I would arrange for the police to be there. In London, it's easier to get the police to be present because they have the manpower. But when you go into rural areas, you're in trouble because they're usually short of men.

I did a gypsy eviction in Guildford once. The constabulary's idea of "police presence" was different from mine. They sent one bobby on a pushbike. He was more concerned about our personal safety than I was; on a gypsy eviction you give them a notice to quit, and a copy of the eviction notice has to be pinned on to the actual caravan. They do not like anything stuck on their caravan door, so that can cause a bit of friction and turn out to be explosive.

There was another case, where I had to serve legal documents to a bus driver. I didn't know what he looked like, but the inspector told me what bus he was driving. So I jumped on to it like a passenger. It was a one-man bus where the driver takes the money. When it came to my turn to buy a ticket, I just served him. He went red, but he could not get out and make a noise about it as there was a bus full of passengers waiting to be transported.

Then I have served a few people summonses while they were having a bath. On one occasion I had to climb up the drain pipe and throw it at the man through the window, because he had been shouting at me through the window and not coming down.

On another occasion, I had my car keys stolen when I was carrying out a surveillance. The guy must have suspected he was being observed and without being noticed he came and nicked the key. I can give anyone doing surveillance some strong advice — "Always have your car doors locked." Fortunately I had a spare key, but it blew that case out of the window.

On another case, I undertook a long observation on a woman. She was an erratic driver. I followed her to Heathrow once from Hyde Park Corner. She was meandering all over the place and I had to keep behind her — it was like a joy-riding exercise for me!

How to recover debts

Patrick: You have done a tremendous job, Ian, in the way you have put across to me all your real-life experiences as a private investigator. How would you sum up your job for the readers, be they company employees or private individuals, and what relevant points should they consider when using a private detective such as yourself to recover money that is legitimately owed?

Ian: There are pluses and minuses in my job. On the minus side, the main drawback is the uncertainty of actually getting the money after all is said and done. And this has been a big issue, particularly in recessionary times.

Pursuing bad debts these days may be a situation of throwing good money after bad.

In pre-recession times, in the 1980s, anyone who owed another under, say, £200 would have been pursued in the ways I have already described to you. But now that figure has changed to £500. And if the amount owed is less, then the chances are it will be written off. People are becoming more discretionary these days, rather than chasing every debt, because in the end it could turn out to be more costly to pursue the matter in every way possible than to just forget it. Nowadays, credit control departments in businesses have become very prominent. There is still emphasis on sales, because that is the lifeblood of business. But companies now realise that getting paid is just as important. That means that greater importance is given to cash flow management because, for a relatively small percentage of what their sale is going to be, they can conduct some basic form of status enquiry, such as: "Do these people live at this address? Are they married or living together? Have they had any County Court judgements? What are their circumstances?" Companies could be saving themselves a lot of time and money. Normally, when the prospective customer is asked to give great detail about their personal and financial circumstances on an application or order form, by employing someone like myself the company can establish in advance whether those statements are true or false, and thereby safeguard themselves.

In the recent recession there has been an increase in genuine cases where people thought with every good intention that they could meet their obligations; but subsequently they have not been able to pay for some reason, and it has had a domino effect. That trend has been increasing throughout the recession. So I suppose uncertainty in getting paid is the main pitfall — one always has to ask oneself "Is it going to be a waste of time in chasing this debtor?"

Patrick: So, even with all your expertise which you use out in the field when chasing debts, there are failures as often as there are successes. And the failures, particularly in bad financial times, could be much greater than the successes.

Ian: Failures are often governed by people's budgets — both my client's and the debtor's. My business is the same as another when it comes to making money. I have to base it on the profit incentive. I can only go so far as my client's budget permits. If I had an open-ended budget I could probably deal with most cases more efficiently by spending more time and money on them to produce a much better outcome, resulting in very few unsuccessful cases. But it is not like that in the real world. You have set budgets. So you do as much as you can for the budget allocated. I don't turn any business away if I can possibly help it. At the outset, I ask my clients how much they want to spend and I will give them the amount of work they have paid for. I am like any other self-employed person — I go to work to earn money. Without being accused of exploiting my clients, I want to make as much profit as I can.

Patrick: So what you are saying is, if they are well-to-do you would hit them with the sledge-hammer! And if they are not that prosperous, you would give them a gentle tap with the mallet!

Ian: I wouldn't say that is quite the case. As it is with all businessmen, I charge what the market can afford — it is a situation of supply and demand. If someone came to me and said they would give me 50 cases a month, I am going to do their work at a much lower rate than I would for another person once in a lifetime. I do not have a golden rule that if someone has the money, I am going to attack them for as much as I can. I don't have to, because people will tell me if they haven't many funds to spend. So I find it much better to let my clients guide me on how much they want to spend. And I always agree a budget ceiling beforehand so that they can't tell me they didn't want to spend so much. If someone wants to spend £10, they will get £10 worth of work. Likewise, if they want to spend £1000, they will get £1000-worth of work.

Patrick: So you would apply that criterion, whether they were an individual or a company?

Ian: Well, 99 per cent of the time I either agree a ceiling, an hourly rate, or a fixed fee for the job. When I agree this beforehand they know what they are getting. Alternatively, if I did send them an invoice without their knowing what sort of figure I was billing them for, that would drive them bananas. I do it this way so that they know precisely what they are spending. In that way there are no arguments. There is only one thing about this profession that I resent, and that is the way in which its image is tarnished by the media — smug people, dirty anorak, snooping around and all that . . . There is still a stigma attached to our profession.

Well, I can tell you it is not that sort of thing at all. These days there are a lot of professional agencies that work from plush offices and have a high profile. My number is in the telephone directory. I do not try to hide from anyone. I work like any other professional person — a solicitor, dentist, accountant or whatever. It is just as necessary a profession as theirs, and will continue to be needed in the foreseeable future. The infrastructure of our society will have to change fundamentally for it to cease to exist.

Patrick: And that is precisely why I wrote **PAY UP!** Debtors and debts will continue to exist as long as our society survives. So we need to know the best way to survive. Thank you once again for the time you have given to this subject.

Individual Voluntary Arrangements (IVAs)

If you end up heavily in debt, or your business has failed, you may opt for an Individual Voluntary Arrangement (IVA).

This is less dramatic than being declared bankrupt, and financial considerations aside, carries less social stigma.

The debtor is usually the only person who can institute an IVA, unlike bankruptcy where creditors may also seek a court ruling. But, if you are an undischarged bankrupt, the Official Receiver may ask for an IVA too.

If your business runs into serious financial problems, you should seek the help of a debt adviser.

He/She will help you assess your position and formulate a financial statement, listing all your debts and assets, and may refer you to an Insolvency Practitioner (IP).

The IP will then decide whether Bankruptcy or an Individual Voluntary Agreement would best suit your personal circumstances. You should consider taking prompt action in case your creditors file to have you declared bankrupt.

Once an Insolvency Practitioner has assessed your financial case, he/she will put together a proposal for the court to consider. But before the proposal can be presented, you must follow a strict methodology to make it legitimate.

If you agree to the terms of the plan, which will account for all your debts and assets and a way of satisfying your creditors, you must formally serve the proposal to your Insolvency Practitioner.

The IP must accept it, then return the signed copy to you the debtor.

After a proposal has been served to an Insolvency Practitioner he/she will become the debtor's "nominee" or court representative.

The debtor can then apply to the court for an "interim order" which, if granted, will provide protection from bankruptcy petitions by any creditors.

If the order is given, the nominee must then present the proposal to the court, usually within 14 days.

This is normally followed by a meeting between the debtor, all creditors and the IP.

Any proposal for an Individual Voluntary Arrangement needs to be approved at a creditors' meeting.

Creditors are given voting rights on the basis of the amount of the debt they are owed.

The proposal must then be supported by 75 per cent of the votes to go ahead.

The plan, which becomes binding, can then be put into action. The Insolvency Practitioner acts as "supervisor" and must notify the court of the result within four days of the meeting.

There are several advantages to the Individual Voluntary Arrangements:

- You are protected from any further action by your creditors.
- Administration is usually cheaper than with bankruptcy.
- Businesses can sometimes continue to operate as a going concern and therefore be sold as such.

Debtors have more say in the decision-making process than they do in bankruptcy cases and are less likely to find themselves at the centre of publicity.

There are several disadvantages to Individual Voluntary Arrangements:

- If the IVA fails, you may still be at risk of being declared bankrupt.
- As with bankruptcy, your credit rating suffers. All IVAs are noted in a public register.
- Your home and other assets are at risk, as with bankruptcy.
- Debts tend to take longer to clear than with bankruptcy, but your creditors may agree to accept a proportion of the money owed.

There are various organisations which may offer useful advice:

- **National Association of Citizens Advice Bureaux**
  115–123 Pentonville Road, London N1 9LZ.
- **Federation of Independent Advice Centres (FIAC)**
  13 Stockwell Road, London SW9 9AV.
- **Money Advice Association**
  Unit 63, Ludgate House, 107–111 Fleet Street, London EC4.

Courtesy BBC Ceefax

Financial hell-holes and how to climb out of them

I met John in January 1994. He was a 35 year-old entrepreneur who in the financial boom period of the roaring '80s was very successful and owned several properties and retail businesses. Here is what happened to him and how he extricated himself from a precarious position. He started his business life by speculating with £5000 in order to accumulate, and also by borrowing more money from the High Street banks. The first business he bought was a laundrette. This was a great success. From there he went on to buy more properties, which he used as collateral to buy more businesses — a bar, restaurant, delicatessen, dance studio and concert promotion company. These businesses were all doing well and giving him a good living. Then things began to go wrong. When the laundrette business started to go down, it had a similar effect on the other businesses because rents and rates went up, VAT went up from 15 to 17.5 per cent, and sales went down with the recession. This trend of events permeated through all of John's businesses and properties and left him

financially crippled and unable to pay his creditors. He had debts totalling £1,000,000. He was harassed by his creditors through the legal channels resulting in court actions and bailiffs visiting him. In his own words, "On one such occasion the landlord of my laundrette business sent in the distress bailiffs to take away my equipment, which to me was the tools of my trade."

John was smart. He read the notice of distress which the two bailiffs had shown him. He realised that the equipment that the bailiffs were trying to take away was the tools of his trade.

The bailiffs insisted that they were going to take it away. John lost his cool, reached for a hammer and smashed it on the countertop as a demonstration of his defiance and anger at their high-handedness. They soon left.

John also received a string of letters from his other creditors demanding payment. He has dealt with them all by offering to pay 1p in the pound using the Individual Voluntary Arrangement (IVA) method for his personal liabilities and liquidation for his limited companies. John, with all his problems, did not go bankrupt and now runs a smart restaurant in a good location. His advice to anyone in difficulty is: "Though you may be undergoing great financial distress and psychological stress — don't give up. I only worry when the banks open for business in the morning. When they close for business in the evening, I close my worry department down! Fight all the way, under all circumstances, and play for time till the situation changes. This should eventually happen if you are patient and don't give up!"

Rags to riches and 49 CCJs

In the search for successful business people who hit a bad patch in their business life and got clobbered financially as a result, and then raised themselves back from rags to riches I met Len — a man who hit rock-bottom and ended up with 49 County Court Judgements (CCJs) for debts totalling £84,000. Here is his amazing life story as he related it to me.

A chequered career

I came to England from abroad in 1974, first got a job and then followed a course in Export studies. I started doing business here in 1984 — ten years ago — and I was 27 years old at the time. I always wanted to do business because I came from a business family background. My great-grandfather started a rollicking bakery business which was handed down over the generations to us, so I guess you could say that business was in my blood! Before I started my own business I did several things. For instance, I worked as a sales rep selling moccasin shoes, leather belts and goods. I arrived in this country almost penniless and my situation was so bad that if I hadn't found a job by the following week, it would have been a different story. But the truth of the matter was that within five years from my humble beginnings I was able to save £5000, which I used as a deposit to buy a house in 1979. Now the house gave me collateral to borrow more money from the bank to start my business. The first business I started was an air freight-forwarding company. From here I moved on to be the general sales agent for air cargo for the airline of my country of origin. My office was on the third floor of a dental practice. Because I was now dealing with air cargo I realised I needed a warehouse to handle the storage facilities. I managed to get a very good location in West London where I built my own 287 sq.ft warehouse with my own money which then cost me £6000. I diversified and expanded, having eight people working for me. I was at this stage also handling sea cargo and road transportation cargo. In fact I became a pioneer in "cargo consolidation" to my country of origin on its national carrier — that is where you buy a large space from the airline and you fill that space with your client's cargo. Because you buy space regularly, you get a better rate from the airline. I started doing this with other airlines too. That was in my heyday. But things began to deteriorate because of severe political troubles that beset my country. War began because of ethnic differences and as a result of it the airline, which was a government concern, could not pay what it owed me on time. Normally the payments would come in between 45 to 60 days, but because of the adverse situation the payment of my invoices got delayed longer than usual. This caused me financial pressure and necessitated my going to the bank to borrow money to keep my business rolling. I did this for six months.

Money problems

This was the beginning of my business decline and the principal cause of its collapse, for when the airline didn't pay me on time I was pressing them because I couldn't pay my creditors who were pressing me, which in turn turned into a negative cycle of events. Because my turnover was so great and I was wrapped up in running the business side, the importance of getting paid on time did not hit me till very late in the day. If as a small company without an in-house accountant to advise you about the position of your credit control on a day-to-day basis, you realise after 180 days that your payment should have been with you 120 days ago, then you have a big problem on your hands. So in our case we had profitability in the business, but in the end the payments were not forthcoming on time and that became a major problem so that great hardship ensued.

This culminated in summons after summons from my creditors. Some of them I managed to settle in part with money I borrowed from various sources. Others I could not, resulting in 49 County Court Judgements against me. Because I went to court for the hearings and explained my case to the court I got easy terms of repayment. While all this was happening it became very difficult for me to run the business because the freight-forwarding industry has its own peculiarities, unlike in (say) a restaurant or hairdressing business: only a few carriers go to certain destinations, and if you don't pay them on time they refuse to handle you. Therefore eventually I had to call it a day.

The remedies

However, I was fortunate in that I had two operations going on at the same time in my business. I dealt with the problem like this. One day I went to my office and did a serious bit of thinking. I realised that although the money was not coming in as required there was a good and a bad side to my business. The good part of the business was where we were doing extremely well with corporate companies, where our outlay was less.

The bad part was where we were doing work for individual clients, who sometimes became very difficult to deal with and who also in certain instances did not pay on time. So I divided the business into the profitable side and the unprofitable side. I formed a new company with the profitable side and sold it, and I wound-up the unprofitable side by going to an insolvency practitioner myself as it was a limited liability company. As a matter of fact, just at the time when I was negotiating with the buyer of my business, in came a bailiff with a court order to remove some of my goods, which incidentally was other people's cargo. So I managed to take him aside and use my charm — I gave him £50 and asked him to call again next week. I knew the bailiff because he had already visited me several times. I told him I was about to sell the business and pleaded with him not to upset the apple cart! The sale went through for £46,000 for goodwill and staff, £18,000 for fixtures and fittings and £25,000 for the building. This gave me enough money to settle with all my creditors and have £5000 profit, with which I immediately went back to my country with my family on a well-deserved holiday.

That was a happy ending which took nearly a year to achieve, but I must tell you it was no fun to have to go through all that hassle. I have been threatened by my creditors with telephone calls such as "If you don't pay us we'll break your legs and arms", and all that sort of stuff. But most of the companies that took me to court knew my past. I always paid them on time and I did have a good payment history with them previously, so they were still reasonably nice to me — even though they took me to court for the money I owed them.

On my personal finances side I lost everything. I had many credit cards at the time... American Express, Barclaycard, Trust House Forte Hotels etc. — they all took their cards away. But because I eventually settled all of them after the sale of my business, I got them all back.

When I was going through with all of this, I was penniless, speechless, sexless, headless and felt worthless. You need a clear head free from distractions to run that kind of business, and when you are being pressed from all sides it just doesn't eat into your business life, it also bites hard into your personal life. I couldn't eat properly because I lost my desire for good food and ate only to survive. I didn't want to meet people because I had no interest in socialising at the time because of my predicament — mind you, 49 CCJs are a big hammer in your head!

Strategy for debtors

How should you deal with an awkward situation when you are being pursued by creditors to whom you owe money is a question that a lot of people would like to have answered by debtors like myself who have been right in the thick of it. The best advice I could give is not to get into that situation — that would be the No. 1 priority. With hindsight, I would say I was a fool. I should have known, when my money was not coming in at the right time, to warn my major creditors of the situation rather than letting them think I was dodging the issue by not paying their invoices and therefore forcing them to take the necessary action to recover their money. So the No. 2 priority is to always inform your creditors — that is an obligation and a courtesy you owe them. Point No. 3 is this. If there is a court action involving payment of money — and this advice I would give to a friend, family member, or anyone else — please don't engage the services of a solicitor! Go to court by yourself, be a "man" and address your adverse circumstances to the judge — the chances are he or she will respect you for it and will be sympathetic towards your case for doing so. Point No. 4 is that if judgement is made against you, they might take a charge on any real property you have. If you are a limited liability company that won't happen because the liability is restricted to your business and does not extend to you personally. But there again, when you go in front of a judge he or she will ask you to give your programme for repayment of the debt and will take into consideration all your existing financial commitments. There are times when you will have to tell the judge, if you have only £5, that you can only afford to give £4, keeping £1 for yourself. And you tell him or her that when you have the money you will pay. If the bailiffs arrive at the the door to collect money or remove goods it can no doubt be embarrassing. But if it is a genuine case and you have not played out anybody, there is nothing you can do about it and that will stand out — you have not done a fraudulent act and the business has got into difficulty so there is not much you can do about it. But having said that, there are a number of debtors who became so because of fraud. If your conscience is clear and you have good motives and are not trying to rob someone, you have nothing to fear and you can endure the hardship — as it was in my case. Having been through all that living hell I can on reflection say that the experience of it has toughened me up and made me a more mature person. You get a lot of confidence when you go through a hardship such as this, and it all happens for the better. What this translates into is that, whether you are making a lot of money in business or losing a lot, you do not over-react to the situation — you treat both the same!

I can now compare my current financial situation favourably with what it once was — for example, earlier on I mentioned I lost all my credit cards, but today I have all the credit cards in my possession — the American Express corporate card, Barclaycard Visa and Mastercard, Access and so on. Now, even though I have all these cards, experience has taught me that having cards is only good for a rainy day — I only use them in exceptional circumstances. I never want to get into a debt situation again and hopefully I will never let it happen again. If I now foresee at any stage any financial shortcomings, I will stop trading straight away. And I will not take any out-of-the-ordinary risks, nor will I borrow money from the banks unless it is absolutely necessary.

From my eight years of trading as a freight-forwarder, the only people who benefited were the banks — they take interest and put a charge on your property and once you get into that situation it is difficult to pull yourself out.

A word of caution to people who are sole proprietors or in partnerships. They have to be very careful. If they have their own houses, vehicles etc., and if they go under, it could be a sad situation because their creditors could take a charge on their assets. When I got judgements against me, my credit rating was affected. I could not borrow any money at the time, which I am now happy was the case. In fact I tried to get a second mortgage on my property, but my building society did not give it. That happened for the best. Now it is all a case of managing my affairs properly, having learnt the hard way.

To sum up, if anybody wants to do business they must have adequate money — that is very essential. If you start borrowing from day 1 it becomes very difficult because the competition is such that they can out-do you if you cannot beat them. If you have sufficient money to see you through for at least six months and if you are professional in your business as well, i.e. you know what you are doing and you do it well, and if you also have the guts to face the difficulties as well as the experience and business acumen, that is the only way forward. In my case I was down and out, but now I am sitting pretty with a variety of businesses and they are all going well in spite of all the day-to-day problems I still have to face. In other words, when you are in business the steering wheel is in your hands and if you want to go to Bristol and you end up in Bath it is your fault. So make darn sure you get it right, right from the start. Business is both sweet and sour, as I found out the hard way.

Fraud and deception

Let us look at Fraud and Deception and their close relatives Cheating, Blackmail, Forgery and False Accounting because, somewhere down the line, wherever the exchange of money is involved there may be elements of fraudulent practice involved to a greater or lesser extent. The *Oxford English Dictionary* describes "Fraud" as: "criminal deception; dishonest trick; person or thing that is not what s/he or it seems or pretends to be." Let us consider various aspects of a situation that could amount to a fraudulent act.

In a "Conspiracy To Defraud" the purpose of the conspirators must be to cause the victim economic loss by depriving him or her of some property or right to which he or she is, or would be, or might become, entitled.

"Cheating" represents deceitful practices in defrauding or endeavouring to defraud another of his/her own right by means of some artful device contrary to the plain rules of common honesty. A possible scenario for such an act could be in a three-card trick or loaded dice in a gambling salon.

"Blackmail" can be alleged if, with a view to gain for themself or another or with intent to cause loss to another, a person makes any unwarranted demand with menaces unless they do so in the belief that they have reasonable grounds for making the demand and that the use of the menace is a proper means of reinforcing the demand.

In "Forgery" the mental element required is that in making, using or possessing the false instrument the villain should intend that the victim should be induced, by means of accepting the false instrument as genuine, to do some act to the prejudice of themself or another.

In "False Accounting" it is required that the villain should intentionally or recklessly conceal, falsify, destroy or deface any account or record of a document made or required for any accounting purpose, or use such a document knowing it is false, and do so dishonestly and with a view to gain for themself or another or with intent to cause loss to another.

In a "Deception" the villain must know that what he or she represents as true is untrue, or with their full knowledge they represent as true that which is not, based on factors which may or may not be true. Thus, if you order a meal in a restaurant knowing that you will not, or cannot, pay for it and having eaten the meal you leave without paying for it, it could be said that you have obtained the meal by deception. Then again, if you have been induced to pay out money to stay in a hotel which has not even been built, and you were led to believe that all was in order, this could be deception.

In one such case, British Rail stewards boarded a train with their own food, which they sold to their passengers instead of supplying them with food provided by British Rail, intending to keep the proceeds of the sale for themselves. The House of Lords decided that they were guilty of a "conspiracy to defraud" British Rail. Likewise, in a legal sense there would be some grounds for saying that they intended to cheat the passengers and to deceive them by obtaining money from sales by deception. You should also be wary of unsolicited telephone calls to tell you that you have won a prize in a draw and that you should come and collect it. The greedy victim may turn up and be told that he or she

will be given the prize after he or she has parted with a sum of money towards an investment in shares or property which may not or never will exist. The victim does not know of this until it is too late.

A friend of mine received such a phone call from a girl and put himself on guard straight away when she was unwilling to give details of the name and telephone number of her employer. He told her point-blank he was not interested in the offer, and he was not bothered by her again.

There are guidelines issued by the Office of Fair Trading for persons selling by telephone printed in the BT phone book under the section "Selling By Telephone". Anyone involved in initiating or making unsolicited phone calls to consumers should read those guidelines. It is well known that in the state of Florida, USA, many people have been induced to part with money as a result of unscrupulous telephone calls.

The large business concern described as "thriving and made of money" usually turns out to be two or three villains working from a shack with a mobile phone and a tape mimicking background business noises. Having made arrangements to receive the money from their victims, the villains simply move to another shack and start again. There was a case where a number of people were invited to invest in a property scheme and were told that for tax purposes and for their own protection the proceeds had been placed in an international bank in the West Indies. One investor became suspicious and investigations revealed that the bank was in fact the back room of a bar of dubious repute. The scheme never existed and the villians had amassed a small fortune before they were tumbled.

As far as Fraud is concerned, I have come across another befitting description — it is the obtaining of a material advantage by unfair or wrongful means. It involves Deception. It involves the making of a false representation knowingly or without belief in its truth, or recklessly.

Fraud and Deception are vast subjects. In this section I have endeavoured to give you an outline of some of the elements that go to make up a fraud. As an individual how do you guard against it? I suggest these precautions:

- Be prudent in your business dealings, and particularly with unsolicited invitations to part with your money.
- Be careful with your possessions, for example credit cards and computer software, and do not let strangers have access to them.
- Do not be tempted into recklessness or foolhardiness by fantastic offers which appeal to the greedy side of your nature.
- Remember, there's no such thing as a free dinner!

No credit?

How to find out what credit reference agencies report about you and how you can correct mistakes

The following information also applies if you are trying to rent a TV or hire something else.

Are you a good credit risk?

Before giving you credit shops and loan companies want to make sure that you're not a bad risk.

They don't have time to ask people who know you so they turn to information-collecting firms called **credit reference agencies,** to get some basic details.

Sometimes loan companies use a system called credit scoring. You "score" points for the information you give on the application form. You can be turned down if you don't get enough points. Because they can use different "scores" you can be rejected by one company and accepted by another.

DID YOU KNOW?

1. You can't have credit as a right.
2. Lenders don't have to say why they've turned you down.

Your rights

If you are trying (or have tried) to get credit for £15,000 or less, you have a legal right to know the name and address of any credit reference agency that was approached for details about you. To find out, simply write to the shop or loan company that refused you credit and ask. But be quick.

- **You must write within 28 days of the last time you contacted them about the credit deal.**
- **They must tell you the name and address within seven working days.**

423 Any Street
Anytown, E43 4KV
20 August 199X

Dear Loan Company

I am writing under section 157 of the Consumer Credit Act 1974. Please tell me the name and address of any credit reference agency which has given information about me. I expect a reply within seven working days of you getting this letter.

Your faithfully

A N OTHER

Details on file

Credit reference agencies don't keep blacklists. They don't give an opinion on whether you should have credit, and they keep information on good payers as well as bad. Agencies simply give out information. It is up to the shopkeeper or loan company to decide whether you are a bad risk.

"X" CREDIT REFERENCE AGENCY	CONSUMER DATABASE
PRESENT ADDRESS: 423 ANY STREET ANYTOWN E43 4KU	PREVIOUS ADDRESS: 234 HIGH STREET ANYTOWN E43 6RS
ELECTORAL ROLL: A.N. OTHER 199X	A.N. OTHER 1986–1989
PUBLIC INFORMATION: NONE	PUBLIC INFORMATION: COUNTY COURT JUDGEMENT £50, COUNTY COURT 1987
PREVIOUS ACCOUNTS: NONE SEARCHES: FILE SEARCHED BY LOAN COMPANY 15/8/9X	PREVIOUS ACCOUNTS: LOAN COMPANY PERSONAL LOAN: £1,000 PAYMENTS: 36 × £40 (ON TIME) SETTLED 12/89
PRESS "E" TO END SEARCH	

Agencies usually keep details of the following:

The electoral or voters' roll. If your address is on the roll this shows that you live at the address given on your application form.
This is very important to a lender.

County Court judgments and bankruptcies. Records are kept of all people taken to court for not paying their debts. Even when a debt has been paid agencies keep a judgment on file for around six years.

In the Scottish Sheriff Court these "judgments" are called **decrees.** The agencies keep details about them for six years in the same way.

Previous Credit Accounts. If you've had credit previously, an agency may have details of how well — or badly — you paid. If you paid on time this is likely to help you get further credit.

Seeing your file

The large agencies keep information about every address in the United Kingdom in their computers. Almost every adult has a "file" — even if there is nothing recorded on it. You don't have to be refused credit to see what information they have about you. You can write to them any time asking for a copy of your file.

You must:

- **send £1 (non-returnable)**
- **give your full name and address (with post code)**
- **give any address you've lived at during the past six years (this helps trace your file).**

It's a good idea to keep copies of any letters you write — you may find them useful later if there's a disagreement about your file entry.

If you run a business give its exact name and address because separate information may be held about you in that capacity.

The agency might ask for more details. Otherwise it has seven working days (starting with the day it receives your letter) to send your file or tell you it has nothing on you.

423 Any Street
Anytown, E43 4KV
1 September 199X

Dear Credit Reference Agency

I am writing under section 158(1) of the Consumer Credit Act 1974. Please send me a copy of my file. I enclose a (postal order/cheque) for £1.

I have lived at the above address for three years. Before that I lived at 234 High Street, Anytown.

I expect a reply within seven working days of you getting this letter.

Yours faithfully

A N Other

THE FOUR MAIN AGENCIES ARE:

CCN Systems Ltd,
Consumer Affairs Dept,
P O Box 40,
Nottingham NG7 2SS

Credit Data and Marketing Services,
CCA Dept, Dove Mill,
Dean Church Lane, Bolton,
Lancashire BL3 4ET

Equifax Europe Ltd,
Consumer Affairs Dept,
Spectrum House,
1A North Avenue,
Clydebank,
Glasgow G81 2DR

Infolink Ltd,
CCA Department,
38 Whitworth Street,
Manchester M60 1QH

Correcting errors

If the facts on your file are correct you can't expect the agency to remove them just because they are embarrassing. Lenders want to know your full credit history, good or bad. If however you feel the entry is incorrect you can ask the agency to change it. Use the following steps.

1. Write to the agency asking it to remove or change any entry which you think is wrong.

Within 28 days the agency should tell you that it will remove or change the entry or take no action.

423 Any Street
Anytown, E43 4KV
14 September 199X

Dear Credit Reference Agency

YOUR REFERENCE: 123456/7890

I am writing under section 159 (1) of the Consumer Credit Act 1974. Thank you for sending me my file. Would you please remove the judgement for £50, or make clear that it was paid in 1988. I enclose my proof of payment. *

I expect a reply within 28 days of you getting this letter.

Yours faithfully

A N OTHER

* Exactly what "proof of payment" is required varies in different parts of the United Kingdom. Ask your local consumer adviser (see "Getting help")

2. **If the agency hasn't replied within 28 days, you can — within 28 days after that — send it a *notice of correction* to add to your file. You can also send such a notice if the agency tells you it will not remove or change the file entry.**

A notice of correction is a statement of up to 200 words. It's your chance to tell your side of the story. What you say is up to you — but the agency can reject your notice if it thinks it is incorrect, frivolous, defamatory or scandalous. Here's an example of a notice of correction.

423 Any Street
Anytown, E43 4KV
28 October 199X

Dear Credit Reference Agency

YOUR REFERENCE: 123456/7890

Thank you for your letter dated 2 October.

I note that you will not remove the entry from my file. Please add the following notice of correction to my file.

NOTICE OF CORRECTION

I, Mr A N Other, would like it to be known that the judgment recorded against me for £50 relates to a bill for my Water Rates. In 1987 I was made redundant and was unable to pay this debt. I paid it after I got a job in 1988. I would ask anyone searching this file to take these facts into account.

I look forward to hearing from you within 28 days of you getting this letter.

Yours faithfully

A N OTHER

What happens next?

If the agency amends your file or adds the notice of correction, it must send the details to anybody who asked about you in the previous six months. The new details must be used in future. If the agency does not want to add the notice of correction it must get the permission of the Director General of Fair Trading. You'll be told if this happens. The agency can refuse your notice if it thinks it is incorrect, frivolous, defamatory, or scandalous.

If the agency doesn't reply to the letter enclosing your notice of correction within 28 days you can ask the Director General to intervene in the dispute.

The Director General has no authority to help you if you have not followed the steps described.

Contacting the Director General

If you have followed all the steps, within the time limits, and you haven't heard from the agency, write to:

The Director General of Fair Trading,
Field House, 15–25 Bream's Buildings,
London EC4A 1PR

Give your full name and address and that of the agency.

Also give:

- **details of the incorrect entry in your file, say why it is incorrect and why you will think you will suffer if the file is not changed;**
- **the date you sent the notice of correction to the agency. If you can't remember give a rough idea.**

To speed things up give all the details you can, such as dates of letters and a copy of your notice of correction and say that you are writing under section 159(5) of the Consumer Credit Act 1974.

The Director General will ask the agency to comment. You will usually see the reply and be asked for your views. The Director General will decide how the matter will be resolved.

423 Any Street
Anytown, E43 4KV
30 November 199X

Dear Director General

I am writing under section 159(5) of the Consumer Credit Act 1974.

I got my file (reference number 123456/7890) from (name of credit reference agency) and asked them to change an entry about my (County Court/Sheriff Court) judgment.
Because they wouldn't take it off my file, I sent them a notice of correction to add to my file explaining why I was taken to court. It is now 28 days later and I have heard nothing.
I believe that if the notice of correction isn't added to my file, it will not be clear why I was taken to court. Please can you contact the agency for me. I enclose copies of all my letters and my file.

Yours faithfully

A N OTHER

Getting help

If you need help with any of these procedures contact your local Trading Standards (or Consumer Protection) Department. The address is in the phone book under your county, regional or borough council. In Northern Ireland the Trading Standards Branch is at the Department of Economic Development.

You can also get advice from a Citizens Advice Bureau or consumer advice centre. See your phone book for the address.

You can also write to the Office of Fair Trading. They may be able to give you some **advice** but if you haven't followed all the steps they've described it is not possible for them to get involved in individual complaints.

(This chapter is reproduced by kind permission of the Office of Fair Trading)

Mental and physical violence in money transactions

Because the subject of getting paid is an emotionally charged topic, mental and physical violence happens all too often. To know the limits on how far both creditor and debtor could go in pursuing and defending their positions before they infringe the law of the land I interviewed Jim, a well-respected criminal lawyer.

What is violence?

Patrick: In business Jim, after a sale is made you will agree with me that the most important thing is getting paid. And if you don't get paid for whatever you have sold, you are in what I call the charity business. In the current economic climate where businesses are crashing at the rate of 1000 every week a number of these businesses have met with their downfall because they couldn't get paid. If you don't get paid you could get into serious financial trouble and meet with the same demise whether you are a small, medium or large business.

Now if you are a creditor in pursuit of your money and you chase it via the telephone or go to see your debtor in person to demand it, at any point in time it could become a very explosive thing because you could lose control and it could lead to you unleashing physical or mental violence on him or her. At what point would you say that such action would constitute mental violence and physical violence?

Jim: It certainly becomes violence when the person who is owed the money goes to collect it and uses threats — both verbal and physical. Because there is a personal interest involved in collecting the money that is owed to someone, that situation is more likely to escalate into violence than him/her sending a third party to collect it.

Obviously if someone is owed money and goes to the other person's house to collect it and sees a nice car or a caravan parked in front, naturally their tempers would start to rise; after all, they are bound to think it is their money which the other person is holding on to and which is giving them a good lifestyle while they have had to suffer the humiliation and detrimental effects of not getting paid. So getting someone else to call on their behalf is one way of defusing the situation.

Patrick: Are you saying that it is wrong to threaten people and ask for money that is rightfully yours?

Jim: Well, if it is rightfully yours you can certainly ask for it — the only thing you can threaten is court action. If you threaten with unlawful violence then it obviously becomes a police matter.

Patrick: In that case, when does the demand become a violent action? — I am referring here to a verbal demand.

Jim: If you tell someone, "Unless you pay me the money by tomorrow you will have your legs broken," then obviously that is a threat involving violence which the law does not encourage and the police could get involved if the victim reports it. If on the other hand you say, "Unless you pay me the money by tomorrow, I will issue proceedings" it may not have the same impact but it is within the law.

Patrick: So you are saying it becomes a serious issue when you threaten physical violence?

Jim: If you threaten physical violence and the person expects you to use that physical violence on them, well yes, that quite clearly involves violence and "threats" can be taken as an "assault". From a criminal law point of view, if you use that sort of behaviour you could be arrested for various offences under the Public Order Act such as for "using threatening words and behaviour".

Patrick: Though that may be the case and should be the norm, I suppose all over the world the authorities at times turn a blind eye to such behaviour because they accept it as another means of collecting money which is owed.
So how on earth could you get someone to pay up if you do not threaten them?

Jim: The only legitimate way, as I told you earlier, is to threaten with legal action which I must admit at times may be unsatisfactory. Some small debt collection agencies that I have known who are actually not qualified, legitimate, certified bailiffs think the best way to collect debts is to send thugs with shaven heads and tattoos and Rottweilers to do the job.

Some small firms behave in the same way — like second-hand car dealers that I have come across in the course of my work. If people buy cars from them and fall back on their agreement, they would without notifying the hire purchase company send a couple of heavies around to tell the debtor: "Make sure your payments are up to date, or else . . .", and it is understood that this was an implied threat suggesting that other action would be taken which might not necessarily be legal action. So without a doubt that sort of thing does take place.

Legal rights

Patrick: Now — say, in response to that action, if someone through fear does pay in part or in full and subsequently decides that they gave the money because they were visited by two brutish looking guys who made implied threats, have they got rights in law to make a counter-claim?

Jim: It depends on the circumstances. If say, a person owes £1000 and pays £500 towards it, they still owe £500. There is a maxim in law that a part-settlement of a debt is no settlement whatsoever — you owe the whole sum — you can't bind someone to take a part of it, because you owe them the whole debt.

Patrick: What I was specifically concerned about here was the threat that was used to get the money. It is agreed that the money is owed. That is not the issue. What is in question is the mannerism used by the creditor to put pressure on the debtor to get the payment. Is it legal or not?

Jim: It is a grey area. The best way I can explain it

is by telling you about a case which actually happened. A company owed money to someone. The guy they owed money to was a burly rough-and-tough second-hand car dealer who used some heavy-handed tactics to get them to pay. They paid up in part. But they resorted to law and put in a counter-claim against the guy for assault in respect of the harassment they suffered. They succeeded to a small extent in getting the overall amount they owed reduced, which they eventually had to pay.

If you do use that sort of violence or threats of violence, it can be an assault or civil assault and it can reduce your claim against the debtor because you will have to pay damages.

But it never really comes to that because people accept that the reason for such actions is that it is a method which the creditor uses to put pressure on them to pay up. It is only when it becomes more serious that the police will get involved when they are asked to.

Patrick: At what point will the police get involved?

Jim: Threats of serious violence and threats to kill. I would say that they may or may not get involved if someone implies violence against you if you told them about it. But if, say, someone came to you and said: "Unless you pay this amount of money by a certain time your legs will be broken" and you believed they would do it, then the police should and would investigate the complaint if it is reported, because that is a criminal offence.

Patrick: And that sort of thing happens often, doesn't it?

Jim: Yes. And few people tell the police.

Telephone threats

Patrick: Let us look now at another area which you can use to put pressure on a debtor to pay up. And that is with the daily used device — the telephone.

With the telephone, as you are not physically confronting the debtor, you can hurl threats and abuse such as, "If you don't pay me I will use your guts for garters as a first instalment and your head as a paper weight as a second instalment and something nasty is going to happen to your family, you son-of-a-bitch." From a criminal angle how is that perceived?

Jim: Certainly from a criminal angle I would advise against it. If the person who is owed the money does act like that, he could find himself falling foul of the criminal law. Even though it is done by telephone, nevertheless the caller is putting fear into the debtor and it certainly will constitute an assault. Over the telephone admittedly it is less direct so the immediacy is gone, but there are all sorts of civil law remedies against harassment like that. The recipient of such calls can get a free-standing injunction against the caller not to pester and harass them. And certainly the debtor can get an injunction against the creditor for behaving like that.

By the way, an injunction is a court order to stop someone from doing something. You can get it for domestic proceedings, harassment, threatening to assault etc. If the perpetrator fails to stop, you can ask the court for a "penal notice". This is used in extreme cases where a warning is given by the court to the person that if he or she breaks a court order again, he or she will be held in contempt of court and therefore will be arrested and committed to prison.

Violence in action

Patrick: Can you give an example of violence used in a money matter?

Jim: Yes, I can. It was to do with the ownership of a house. What it meant was that the owner of a house had to sell the property or pay a certain amount of money to his sister for her share of it. The firm of solicitors I worked for represented his sister. We took him to court and got judgement for him to pay us a certain amount for his sister's share of the property. He felt that the legal action was misconceived and thought it a big disgrace that the matter had to go to court and that he was ordered to pay this large amount of money. He couldn't pay because he was not working. He realised that if he couldn't pay the money to us then he could possibly lose the house.

He wrote to us and and various other people saying that if we made him lose his house he would lose his livelihood.

He then concluded that if he lost his livelihood it would effectively mean he lost his life, because it wouldn't be worth living. And he told us that if we let that happen he would make our solicitor, for whom I was working as an articled clerk at the time, lose his life.

In the circumstances the solicitor contacted the police straight away because we were due to take possession of the property in three days' time. This man quite clearly was issuing a death threat against our solicitor — a partner in the firm.

What happened next was that a bailiff turned

up at the house with us and the police, but the man refused to leave. So we had to go to court again to try and get him out. He continued to issue more death threats to the solicitor and even put it in a personal letter saying he would take his life. So eventually the police had to arrest him and get him out.

In legal terms he was clearly violating the law, but because our firm did not want him to go to prison or to take any further action against him we just sought the support of the police to prevent a breach of the peace.

Patrick: Do you know of any cases where in the pursuit of money people have been physically assaulted, or near to it?

Jim: Yes. There was a case to do with the hire purchase of a car. The finance company that lent the money was involved. As you may already know, a lot of these companies provide credit at extortionate rates of interest.

Our client got the car through the finance company, while knowing he had a long-standing illness. The car salesman who sold him the car told him not to worry about his ill health as the scheme would take care of the payments. But it didn't.

He kept the car in the drive. He received threatening letters from the finance company to which he didn't respond. A few days later he had his car windows smashed in. But there was nothing that the police could tie in with the finance company. Then two days later two hoodlums turned up. They said: "We are very sorry to hear what has happened to your car, but it is not as bad as what is going to happen to your face if you don't keep up with your payments." So our client slammed the door in their faces. But two days later they were back again — this time with baseball bats and

threatening him to pay up. And these guys did not look like baseball players. For reasons best known to them, I suppose, they were visiting our client for baseball practice!

Again, when his car got damaged for a second time he felt he had had enough and contacted us. We then wrote to the finance company and said: "Look, there is something going on here. You should check who you are using to collect your debt. We strongly disapprove of it. And we shall quote the incidents if you sue our client." From then on the harassment stopped. Then there was another case we handled. Our client was not as pure as driven snow, by any means. This, too, had to do with a hire purchase agreement: the finance company sent heavies around to his door when he failed to keep up the payments and he got involved in fisticuffs with them — he thought he would happily get stuck in and have a little fun on his own doorstep, so he had a good punch-up with them and gave them back a bit of their own medicine. He did not report the matter to the police and neither did we.

Patrick: Physical violence as displayed in that incident could turn into something more serious. Have you also heard of any stabbings and shootings as a consequence of money owed, much as we come across every now and then in the media?

Jim: There was one I heard about some time ago. It involved two second-hand car dealers from south London. The first dealer bought cars and sold them on to the second dealer, who also dealt in scrap metal. Because the two parties concerned were both used-car dealers, it was more of a heavy league type of car trade activity. The second dealer owed money to the first, who took a very serious attitude towards collecting his money. The first company had a big turnover and used to finance their car deals through a finance company. So when they didn't get their money, they sent thier own staff with guns to use as a lever to collect it. And because they were armed they got the money very quickly. Within the second-hand car trade, if people don't pay up, it is viewed very seriously.

There was another case where stolen cars were being sold on and a knife was used to threaten a person to make him pay up. The code of practice within the used-car trade is that the loser loses out, but everybody down the chain must get paid. And I have been discreetly informed that if anyone down the line doesn't pay up, the garage concerned makes darn sure that they do. So, in other words, they enforce their own code of honour.

Nowadays when individuals get into debt, for example clients with whom I deal, it is more a case of physical violence that is threatened (rather than carried out) by their creditors, who also try to make life difficult for them.

Patrick: Do people go so far that they not only try to take revenge on the debtor by trying to harm him physically, but also his family and property?

Jim: Certainly the property can get damaged or threatened to be damaged. Sometimes there are threats to the family. But more often there are threats to the debtor that if he doesn't pay up, he will get beaten up.

Patrick: Do some of the big, the so-called "respectable", companies also resort to these tactics? Do they have a dirty tricks department that operates clandestinely?

Jim: I haven't come across any. I'm not saying they don't. The finance companies that I deal with appear to be respectable. They say that they don't employ heavies and it is the garages that do those sorts of things because it is the garages who offer their customers the finance agreements. Those illegal activities are more likely to be carried out by the garages who desperately want to get paid by any means, and dodgy back-street traders. After all, getting paid is paramount to their survival.

Patrick: If we were to take another scenario: suppose a prostitute offers certain services to a client and the client refuses to pay, it is natural

that prostitutes too can go crazy and become physically violent and abusive — we know that happens regularly in many sleazy joints all over the world. After all, it is business, and they are human too. What are your comments?

Jim: Correct. That is why they have pimps to take care of that side of the business. It is the same as the clip joints in Soho. There are bouncers on the door to make sure that people who enter do pay up. And I have heard stories that once in, if a customer refuses to pay for anything offered or even question it, the bouncers are quickly on the scene and take the person by force to the nearest cash-point with one arm behind their back, put them against the wall, take the money from their pockets and then throw them out.

Patrick: Wouldn't that be extortion?

Jim: Definitely. But it is trading on embarrassment because people don't want to report it to the police.

Guidelines for creditors and debtors

Patrick: Would you now like to give me a list of things that people should not do to infringe the criminal law, and also a list of things people can do if they are being threatened with or undergoing mental or physical violence as a result of a money problem? In other words, looking at it from both the creditor's and debtor's standpoint, what is the most effective way of pursuing the payment and also staying within the law?

Jim: Let me do it in point form.

1. What you must always do is tell the person who owes you the money that it is legitimately yours, that they are in breach of the contract and that they have a legal obligation to pay you the money. If they don't respond, you can threaten them with legal action.
2. I would make sure that the person who owes you the money knows that you are taking it very seriously, that you are not going to back off and that you will take it as far as it can go. Always keep applying the pressure through letters of demand, and telephone calls. But if that doesn't

work, the court is the place to resolve the problem. It can be slow, cumbersome and costly and I admit sometimes it does not produce the desired solution, but I am afraid it is the only legal way out in the circumstances. But before you embark on court action you must know whether the person you are pursuing is worth anything and has the necessary assets.

3. The criminal law is such that anything could be interpreted as a criminal offence if you use threatening words or behaviour. For example, if you shout at someone in the street, it can easily come under the heading of a criminal offence because you were using threatening words or behaviour.

   If you intend a person to think that violence is on its way or even if he or she just thinks violence is on its way, then using aggressive language can be an offence.

4. If you are being visited by heavies with baseball bats terrorising you on top of the financial distress you are undergoing as a result of your inability to pay, for your protection and peace of mind call the police immediately. If they can't do something to your satisfaction, try getting an injunction taken out against the people you suspect are responsible for such actions.

   I might mention here that you can only use force back in self-defence if you think you are going to be assaulted — as an instant reaction or with the minimum amount of lawful force needed to prevent yourself from being assaulted. If someone came to your doorstep and used threatening words or behaviour you wouldn't normally be allowed to drag them into your home and beat the living daylights out of them . "In self-defence" means that you are allowed to prevent an attack on yourself by reasonable means. You are allowed to use reasonable force to protect yourself in the circumstances. If they have baseball bats, then you would be allowed to use something stronger to protect yourself than if they came with twigs. The two offences I was talking about earlier fall under sections 4 and 5 of the Public Order Act. They are quite interesting because by law they are only considered to be offences if they happen anywhere other than in a person's own home.

So if someone came and used unlawful threatening words or behaviour and it happened outside your own doorstep and you then took them in and threatened them, it wouldn't be an offence against section 4 or 5 of the Public Order Act, but it can still constitute an assault.

But the main thing you should aim to do is to get them out of the house. You can use reasonable force to get them off your premises. By coming into your premises, they are committing a civil offence — trespassing (which is not a criminal offence). If they do it again, the police have to be involved. And you can take a civil action against them and get an injunction, if you know who they are. The police may take criminal action against them for harassment and for pestering you.

5. The two main offences under the Public Order Act are described in sections 4 and 5. They are both tried in the Magistrate's Court. Section 5 carries a penalty of only

a fine, but not imprisonment, for minor cases involving threatening words or behaviour. Under section 4, where serious threats or behaviour are involved you could be locked up for six months. And that will be followed by a criminal record.

Patrick: How serious is a criminal record?

Jim: It is very serious. It can ruin your job prospects because a lot of employers take notice of it. It shows you have been in trouble with the police. Many employers would require you to show them that you haven't been in trouble for the past five years before they would even consider you.

A criminal record also shows you have broken the law, and people do not consider you trustworthy. There was one guy who was taken to court — it had nothing to do with money. He swore at a traffic warden, calling her all the names under the sun and he ended up with a fine and a criminal record because of it. There was no physical violence involved. People do not realise that using obnoxious language can be a criminal offence. And that is an area of criminal law that you can easily transgress in a state of anger or worry over money matters. You can imagine in such situations people saying, "Give me the f...... money, you bastard, or you will get so-and-so."

The police tend to use common sense in such cases. They often try to calm people down and send them away if it's a first occurrence. But if it is repeated, then they will take action.

Loan sharks

Patrick: Are there any more points that come to mind on this topic regarding the criminal law?

Jim: The only other situation I can think of is where people borrow money on credit and are unable to pay. The lenders go around to these people, who are not so well off and yet who, despite their precarious financial situation, borrowed money at exorbitant rates of interest. A lot of the money lenders or loan sharks collect every week — say £2 per week. It is that sort of person who is not a licensed credit broker who can make life a misery for their debtors.

Every week, like clockwork, they knock on the door expecting money, and it is from those quarters that threats tending towards violence emanate. They terrorise their debtors by turning up late at night; they may take items of jewellery in lieu of payment at ridiculous rates — for a fiver, for example, they may take items of jewellery from the wife worth a lot more. They play on people's weaknesses — when the husband is out, they call on the wife and put pressure on her to pay. It is easier to pressurise a woman into paying money, so they take advantage of a situation when they can.

These loan sharks are ruthless people. To pay a weekly pittance of an instalment they may make people pawn their goods, or they take the debtor's belongings as security to pay for the loan and sky-high interest rates which they charge.

I would like to point out quite clearly that if someone is getting repeated visits, or letter after letter, or relentless phone calls demanding payment, it can become incredibly stressful. Therefore this person needs to take control of the situation and fight back as outlined above — the sooner the better. Let me give you an example. There was a double-glazing firm who sold their product to a little old man who was partially blind. They would go to his house almost every day and demand money, and they would harass him by night with phone calls. We represented this man and told the company that they should go to court if they wanted the money that desperately. And we told them that if they didn't stop pestering him, we would take them to court with a civil action against them, and put in a counter-claim for damages for harassing and pestering the old man which would greatly reduce the money owed to them. They stopped troubling him — they realised that this aggressive behaviour could be counter-productive because our actions could rip up the debt.

If people are involved in such situations and can go and see a solicitor, then they can make use of their creditor's unsavoury actions against them. People would say it is probably not fair that this man got away with £6,000 worth of windows for £600. It is also quite possible that the double-glazing company has written off the debt because they would have realised that if we stood up in court and said that this old man was harassed by them it would not have done their reputation any good — particularly if the media got to know about it. We have not heard from them now for a long time.

Patrick: So it just goes to show that if you are being pursued, the people who are chasing you can gain the upper hand over you if you do nothing. All you will have to show for it is fear and worry. Whereas, if you fight back with legal weapons, you stand a good chance of coming out of it all the better.

Jim: That is right. People get away with a lot of things because their victims don't go and see solicitors or report the matter to the police, or won't take action themselves.

If, on the other hand, you do fight back, you stand a better chance of coming out of the predicament in good shape.

The court's attitude

Patrick: Do courts tend to support the creditors or the debtors?

Jim: By and large they tend to sympathise more with the people who owe the money.

I did a case once in which a man owed a bank £30,000. I was there at the hearing and suggested that the man pay the bank so much a week. And the judge said, "Yes — what is the point of making people bankrupt these days? It would do the man or society no good."

It worked out that it would have taken the man 75 years to pay back the debt. He was 59 years old. The court made an order for him to pay £10 per month, knowing full well that he could never pay back the money before he died. So the bank — one of the Big Five — had to be content with that judgement.

When businesses are going down at the rate of a 1000 a week and the finacial situation in the country is gloomy, people are finding themselves in desperate financial situations. So, if someone makes an offer which is the best he can afford, the courts tend to accept it nowadays as the best solution in the circumstances.

Patrick: Suppose you were to avoid the criminal offence aspects of pursuing the money, such as using threatening words and behaviour or physical violence to scare the debtor into paying. Say for example, you have done business with someone, and for reasons beyond their control they could not pay you. Suppose you were to apply the humane approach to it and told your debtor: "Look, Mr So-and-So, we did business in good faith and on good terms, but unfortunately things didn't work out for you — hence you're in this financial quagmire. Sort yourself out, and pay me when you can."

Don't you think this is a much better way of solving the problem than creating a hornet's nest for yourself and the debtor?

Jim: It all depends on who it is, because some people will obviously try and take advantage of the situation and refuse to pay, as in the case of the seasoned debtor, who will just laugh at you and take you for another ride.

I know one person who was a professional debtor. He very craftily put everything he had in his wife's name a long time ago — long enough ago for the courts not to think he did it recently just to get himself out of owing people money. He would quite happily make purchases for £10,000 to £15,000 at a time. People wouldn't check whether he had the money or not. And he would just say to them, "Sue me, I have no money!" He took them for an absolute ride and would just laugh in their face. There was nothing they could do because he had absolutely no assets and no income, and was signing on the dole.

Patrick: If you were to sum up the whole concept of violence in the pursuit of money, how would you put it in a nutshell?

Jim: Violence is counter-productive. If the person who is receiving the threats realises what options he has and takes them, it would always look bad for the person who is carrying out the threats. It could involve criminal pro-

ceedings with the likelihood of a criminal record which can't do anybody any good.
The alternative must therefore be forceful action within the framework of the law.

How to get your money — a summary

This book has given a variety of approaches for getting paid. Here is a summary of what I consider to be the most effective methods you can use to get your money.

Whatever method you use, it is your choice and your responsibility. Also, do not fail to study the psychology and communication skills, found in my two other books, **WHO DARES SELLS** and **PITCH & GET RICH.** They are both imperative and invaluable aids to getting paid.

1. Be persistent in asking for your money.
2. Be humorous, even when the situation is not in your favour.
3. Threaten with legal action, but don't necessarily take it. If you have to sue, then you must do so and hope for the best.
4. Try to spot if a potential customer is shifty through their body language. If he/she shows signs of deception, don't make unnecessary trouble for yourself, unless you are skilled at handling that type of person.
5. Always empathise — don't sympathise.
6. Listen carefully.

7. For a customer who is undergoing genuine difficulty in paying you, have a constructive plan to show your debtor how he can pay you off.
8. Be fair and firm in your dealings.
9. Be positive.
10. Be honest, patient and kind.
11. Always use wisdom, bearing in mind that a debtor, like yourself, is also another one of God's creatures and we have to show love and mercy to our adversaries if we are to expect the same in this life and in the next.
12. If you decide to use a debt collection agency to do the dirty work and get you your payments, they can use a combination of activities such as tracing, telephoning, letter-writing and door-knocking to pursue the debtor on your behalf. Whether you use a debt collection agency or not is a matter of personal choice.
13. Don't be afraid to use the available legal procedures. If in doubt, see a solicitor.

There you have a comprehensive package, the methodology and philosophy for getting paid. Use it with confidence and you will not lose out. And people will **PAY UP!**

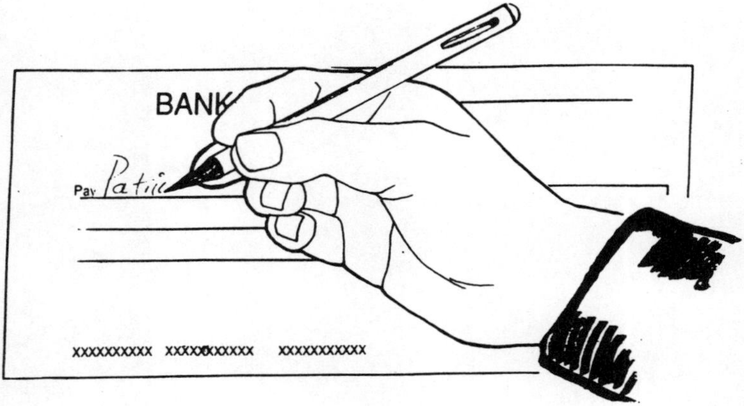

Professional training on how to sell products, services or ideas effectively, and get paid is provided by the author. For further information please contact Patrick Ellis at:

WHO DARES SELLS Publications,
12 Alexandra Court,
Lampton Road,
Hounslow,
Middlesex TW3 4DL,
United Kingdom.
Tel: 081-572 2289
Fax: 081-572 2289

Index

OTHER BOOKS

By Patrick Ellis

PITCH & GET RICH

THE WORLD'S SECOND-OLDEST SELLING PROFESSION!

This unique publication identifies and analyses some of the mind-bending techniques used in the world's oldest and most effective form of pure selling, namely pitching.

It brings together two of the world's most skilful and respected salesmen, combining their exceptional talents to provide more winning secrets for selling and buying success.

Together with Patrick Ellis' **WHO DARES SELLS, PITCH & GET RICH** gives the reader the ultimate winning formula for super-selling and buying in any part of the world.

The Contents include:

- The History of Pitching
- The Philosophy of Pitching
- Pitching vs Modern-Day Selling
- The Elements/Styles of a Pitch
- and much more . . .

Tony Jordan started working on open markets at the age of 18. He went on to become one of the U.K.'s leading pitchers. After a decade of pitching, he organised and conducted the only training course in the country to introduce the "Art of Pitching" to salespeople from different backgrounds.

Since retiring from market trading he has gone on to become one of the country's popular television scriptwriters for the BBC and ITV, working on such acclaimed series as *East Enders, Minder, Boon* and *Trainer*.